Confessions of a Prison Chaplain

Mary Brown

Foreword Juliet Lyon

❧ WATERSIDE PRESS

Confessions of a Prison Chaplain
Mary Brown

ISBN 978-1-909976-04-7 (Paperback)
ISBN 978-1-908162-73-1 (Epub ebook)
ISBN 978-1-908162-74-8 (Adobe ebook)

Cover design © 2014 Waterside Press. Design by www.gibgob.com. Cover image 'Imprisonment' by 'David' whilst serving as a prisoner at HM Prison Acklington © 2010, courtesy the Koestler Trust. Maggi Hambling Highly Commended Award 2010. Photograph of Mary Brown taken by and Copyright © 2014 Noel Baker.

Main UK distributor Gardners Books, 1 Whittle Drive, Eastbourne, East Sussex, BN23 6QH. Tel: +44 (0)1323 521777; sales@gardners.com; www.gardners.com

North American distribution Ingram Book Company, One Ingram Blvd, La Vergne, TN 37086, USA. Tel: (+1) 615 793 5000; inquiry@ingramcontent.com

Cataloguing-In-Publication Data A catalogue record for this book can be obtained from the British Library.

Printed by CPI Antony Rowe, United Kingdom.

e-book *Confessions of a Prison Chaplain* is available as an ebook and also to subscribers of Myilibrary, Dawsonera, ebrary, and Ebscohost.

Published 2014 by
Waterside Press
Sherfield Gables
Sherfield-on-Loddon
Hook, Hampshire
United Kingdom RG27 0JG

Telephone +44(0)1256 882250
E-mail enquiries@watersidepress.co.uk
Online catalogue WatersidePress.co.uk

Dedicated to all Children of God in our prisons.

If you are opening this then you are a nonce ai ai die

We ransack the heavens,
the distance between
stars; the last place we look
is in prison, His hideout
in flesh and bone.

From 'The Prisoner', by R S Thomas

Contents

About the Author

Mary Brown has spent time in three very different prisons: a woman's prison, where she was an inmate on remand for ten days in 1960, following a peace demonstration; an open prison where she was a teacher in the 1980s; and latterly where she was a Quaker prison chaplain for some ten years at the start of the 2000s. She is the author of the Waterside Press publication *Inside Art* (2001).

The Author of the Foreword

Juliet Lyon CBE is Director of the Prison Reform Trust, General Secretary of Prison Reform International and one of the UK's leading commentators on penal matters.

Foreword

In this engaging, thought-provoking book we enter the closed confines of prison, a place of conformity, through the personal account of Mary Brown, non-conformist and Quaker prison chaplain. Going inside we get a sense of a noisy yet isolated, uncertain yet predicable, environment and what it might feel like to be 'banged-up'.

Does it help to know, as it turns out Mary does, what it's like to be the other side of that metal, clanging door without keys? She writes that she will never forget the 'degrading, dehumanising process of reception'. Her reflections on the nature of power and powerlessness, as experienced in the day to day interactions of prison life, raise important questions about how you set about making prisons places of decency and humanity.

Her observations lead you to share the frustration about petty rules and bureaucracy but also to learn about the small kindnesses and rays of hope you glimpse in prison. You gain insights about relationships between prisoners and between prisoners and staff. Mary describes the growing use of restorative justice which offers more hope than most things.

Through her writing you hear snatches of conversation and voices behind bars. Mary introduces quotes and sayings that, in Quaker parlance, 'speak to your condition'. With a light touch she quotes from, amongst others, Solzhenitsyn, John Donne and *Quaker Advices and Queries*. At one point she refers to Winston Churchill's seminal speech in 1910 in the House of Commons about imprisonment and civilisation.

Later in that same speech Churchill warned:

> 'We must not forget that when every material improvement has been effected in prisons, when the temperature has been rightly adjusted, when the proper food to maintain health and strength has been given, when the doctors, chaplains and prison visitors have come and gone, the convict stands deprived of everything that a free man calls life. We must not forget that all these improvements, which are sometimes salves to our consciences, do not change that position.'

From this book, you do not feel that Mary became a prison chaplain to salve her conscience but rather because of her belief in 'that of God in everyone' and because it was her way to 'foster the spirit of mutual understanding and forgiveness' referred to in *Quaker Advice* No. 22. In turn, her confessions contribute to our understanding of the hidden, often neglected world of prison. She sets out so clearly from her perspective how loss of liberty is the punishment of imprisonment and why no one should underestimate the impact of that loss—both during, and long after release or indeed retirement from, prison.

Juliet Lyon

Preface

'Respect the wide diversity among us in our lives and relationships ... Remember that each one of us is unique, precious, a child of God.'

Quaker Advices and Queries No. 22

I have been in three very different prisons: a women's prison, where I was an inmate on remand for ten days in 1960, following a peace demonstration; an open prison where I was a teacher for about five years in the 1980s; and a prison where I was a Quaker chaplain for some ten years at the start of the 21st-century. The majority of this book concerns the last of these, but there are brief chapters on the other two experiences. I am not identifying the prisons, I call the prison where I was an inmate 'W prison' (a women's prison), the open prison I call 'D prison' (open prisons are D category, the lowest level of security) and the prison where I was a chaplain is 'B prison' (a local prison, B category — not the highest level of security, but men were locked up most of the day. Prison W was also B category).

In B prison I was appointed as a Quaker chaplain. Quakers are a small denomination, which grew out of the religious ferment around the time of the civil war in the 17th-century. George Fox, the founder of Quakerism, was a Christian, dissatisfied with the church of his day; he went through great spiritual turmoil and searching, before being able to write that he heard a voice saying, 'There is one, even Christ Jesus, that can speak to thy condition.' Quakers believe this today, thus we have no clergy or priests. We meet in silence waiting to hear the voice of God. These silent meetings are called 'meetings for worship.' Anyone, who feels they have a message for the meeting is free to speak. This is called 'ministry.' Quakers are also known as The Society of Friends, and members as Friends; here I use the terms Quaker and Friend interchangeably. Today not all Quakers call themselves Christian, and few of these, I suspect, would believe in a bodily resurrection. There are Quakers who belong also to other Christian denominations or faiths. There is also a Quaker Universalist Group, testifying to the truth of all religions.

Quakers have no creed, beyond the belief in 'that of God in everyone' or 'God in all,' some preferring to call it 'the Inner Light'. We try to live our lives in the spirit of this belief, which is the basis of our commitment to work for peace, and in social service of many kinds, including ministry to those in prison. This is also the basis of our four 'testimonies': to truth, to peace, to equality, and to simplicity. Early Friends were prepared to die for these. We also have a booklet called 'Advices and Queries' from which these are read from time to time in our meetings, and which I made frequent use of in silent prison meetings.

I was nominated by my Quaker monthly meeting as a Quaker prison minister. Both these terms have changed, and we now have area meetings (which deal with the business side of several local meetings) and Quaker prison chaplains (QPCs). I have used the up to date terms throughout the book Quaker chaplains are nominated by their area meetings, but appointed nowadays by the Ministry of Justice.

Shortly after I retired, B prison was closed in the interests of economy. It must have been expensive to heat in winter, and had a relatively large staff for around 250 prisoners. So it might have seemed wise economics to close it. But it had a friendly atmosphere, relationships between officers and pris-oners were relaxed; many of the men I met there said it was the best prison they had been in. I have heard similar things said of other prisons that have been closed. I suspect this goodwill may be lost in a large, 'Titan', prison.

I got to know many prisoners in my time in B prison, but I have changed all their names, with the exception of Charlie (see *Chapter 5*). He was the original inspiration for my previous book on art in prisons, *Inside Art*, and was adamant that he didn't want a pseudonym: he was Charlie and proud of it. He would have liked his surname used as well.

None of the other men quoted in the book is any particular man: some are a combination of different people, some men I have made into more than one person to hide their identities. Some are just invented names to attach to things I was told, but where I cannot remember who said them or why. If I name no members of staff; this is partly because the book is mainly about my relationships with prisoners, not because I don't see the staff as 'children of God' which of course they are. Most of my time in the prison, however, was spent with the prisoners.

CHAPTER ONE

Portrait of a Prison

'Her Majesty's Prison Service serves the public by keeping in custody those committed by the courts. Our duty is to look after them with humanity and help them lead law-abiding and useful lives in custody and after release.'

HM Prison Service Mission Statement as displayed in all prisons

We all know what a prison looks like from innumerable films and television programmes: what it feels like is harder to convey. It obviously feels different for those who are there as members of the prison staff, and those whom society has sent there to be locked-up. For those who are there for the first time and those who have been there many times before, for whom it may almost be a home: the short-term prisoner and the lifer. Similarly for uniformed and non-uniformed staff. I can only write of how it is for me, going in every Monday morning.

I go into B prison through double electronically locked doors: the inner door cannot be unlocked until the outer is locked. For a few seconds those going there to work are trapped between the two doors. I find this disturbing, claustrophobic: even staff are briefly locked in. Emerging from the doors, I hand my 'tally', a circular metal disc, worn thin by years of use, to an officer and am given a set of keys in exchange. Prisoners must never see the keys, they might be able to memorise the design and forge them. There are No.1 and No.2 keys for opening different doors, and a smaller cell door key. I seem to have a problem with keys, often managing to get them tangled in the chain attached to my belt which is how they must be kept at all times.

Locking and unlocking. Unlocking and locking. You don't lock a cell door with the key, but by banging the door shut with a clang unique to prison. Men say they are 'banged-up'. Banged-up. Banging, banging, banging. The prison echoes with the sounds of imprisonment, which are impossible to shut out. Prisoners are constantly reminded, day and night, that their lives are no longer their own; they're locked in. Banged-up.

'You can't sleep in here for the noise,' says Joe, 'you've got inconsiderate neighbours playing their loud music, officers stamping round, banging doors and jangling keys. They do it deliberately to stop us sleeping'.

I don't like to suggest that perhaps it's just that the landings weren't designed to be walked along quietly, and the officers are only doing their night time duties.

'When men complain that I lock them up, I always say, "Keys unlock as well as lock",' said an experienced chaplain when I was a novice. I didn't reply. It's surely better to do your own locking and unlocking. A prison chaplain may unlock prisoners, but must always relock them, or they would soon lose their job. Perhaps no-one should work in a prison who hasn't experienced being on the other side of the door, without the keys.

Now I am into the strange world of prison: difficult to explain to those who haven't been there. Like the past, it's a foreign country, they do things differently. Locking up one's fellow human beings is not a very human or humane thing to do. The prison atmosphere seems to be permeated with mistrust. Security is the chief concern for all who work there, even for chaplains.

I walk through this typical Victorian prison (actually dating from 1792), with its three stories of landings arranged round a vast emptiness. The suicide nets slung across this void are disturbing, a constant reminder of just how grim life in prison is. They seem to say to the men, 'However dreadful it is here, ending your life is not an option.' Every officer carries a 'fish knife', so-called because it's shaped like a fish, and specially designed to cut down a prisoner who has tried to hang himself. A chaplain in another prison told me that there chaplains also carried fish knives. I'm glad we don't here.

Every prison telephone has the number of The Samaritans above it, who can be rung free. There is also the Listeners service, where prisoners are trained and supervised by Samaritans to listen to the problems, the despair of others. I meet several Listeners, and am impressed.

'This isn't something I've ever done before,' says George, 'it's changed me. I'd never have thought of doing it. One of the screws suggested it. I'd like to go on doing something like this when I get out.'

Others told me of being saved by a Listener. Yet when I suggest to Robert that he might talk to one, he says, 'I wouldn't talk to a con.' Nevertheless most do, and it helps both parties. Much informal helping also goes on in the prison. Many supportive relationships develop between men as they listen to one another's problems in discussions after our silent meeting.

The whole prison seems claustrophobic: locked doors, key chains hanging from the belts of all members of staff, cramped conditions. Even on 'association', when men are allowed out of their cells to play table-tennis or snooker, or just chat, the atmosphere is still of containment, restriction. Thinking of how the prisoners manage to cope with living in this atmosphere, I climb stairs, open and relock many sets of double doors, walk along landings past cells, trying not to look down at those nets, and finally reach the chapel. This is a large space, with a high ceiling, it seems the only place in the prison where there is some relief from the sense of oppression.

George says, 'When I go to the chapel, I feel better, just for being there, it's the space, it reminds me of freedom.'

Yet I feel a sense of the Victorian hell-fire still lurking here. I unlock the chaplaincy office and listen to the messages on the answering machine: who has rung with what problems since last a chaplain was there? Perhaps I hear the voice of a chaplain in the nearby women's prison with a message for the partner of one of their prisoners; or perhaps a reply to a message sent by a chaplain here to that prison; the answer to some query by a government department, but I'm not sure what the question was; a message from a relative, or an officer requesting a visit to someone; a tearful relative reporting a death, almost inaudible through tears — sometimes it's hard to hear the name of the prisoner, or the name of the caller so I have to listen again, and again. Then I read through the Day Book, to see what's happened since I was last here, what problems are left for me to try to help to solve.

I must also study carefully the book issued by Security, updated weekly, illustrated with photographs of men who might be a security risk. If there are two men who might get into a fight if they met, they will be housed on different wings, and we must never have both in the chapel at the same time. Chapel is one place where men on different wings can meet, and we have to be careful. We're expected to read this book each week. Some of the entries concern men who've made threats against staff members, or who have a history of inappropriate behaviour towards women. I'm often surprised to see some names in that book, men whom I've met and found to be caring and considerate. However, most of the men I meet appear to be reasonable and harmless; polite and respectful. From overhearing conversations, I know they frequently use expletives, but in chapel they try not to swear, apologising if the F-word comes out, and reprimanding each other.

'Don't speak like that to the chaplain,' says Don.

'It doesn't matter,' I say.

'Yes it does.'

Then I start on the statutory duties or 'stats.' If there's more than one chaplain in that day we share these. They are prescribed by the prisons department, for chaplains to do each day. They include visiting everyone in healthcare or in solitary confinement, visiting all new prisoners within 48 hours of their arrival at the prison and anyone who asks to see a chaplain. These requests may come on an official form, or informally when an officer says, 'John wants to see a chaplain', or sometimes, 'I think John needs to see a chaplain.' Sometimes you meet John on the landing and he says, 'Can I have a word.'

A visit to a prisoner can vary from someone wanting a Bible, through a complaint that he has failed to have dealt with satisfactorily by staff or a member of the Independent Monitoring Board — usually there is nothing a chaplain can do about this, beyond suggesting a request to see the governor — to a severe social or emotional problems: a 'Dear John' letter bringing bad news, the death of a friend or relative, help with writing a letter, which the prisoner wants to keep confidential. I can never know how long such visits will take; there's seldom a day when someone in the prison doesn't want to see a chaplain. It may take the rest of the morning, and can involve all kinds of problems, misery, humour or just friendly chats.

Visiting those in healthcare I find hard. Most have mental health problems, and many are completely deluded.

'See those pipes?' says Alexander, pointing to the central heating system in his cell, 'that's where they are. Spying on me.'

'That's hard for you,' I say, remembering a mental health awareness course: we should neither collude with nor contradict such delusions. But it makes conversation hard.

One day, as usual, I ask the officer in healthcare, 'Is there anyone you think would like to see a chaplain, or shall I just wander around?'

'We don't need a chaplain, no one's dying here at the moment.' I don't know if he's just new and doesn't understand we have to come each day, or if he means it to be offensive or a joke. I wander about the place as usual.

When opening a cell door I have to firmly strike the bolt with the edge of my hand, which locks the door open, so I can't be trapped inside with the prisoner or prisoners. There are stories of chaplains who forgot this, and accidentally got locked in. This never happened to me, but banging the bolt is quite painful to the hand so, if I have only a brief message to pass on, perhaps a Bible to deliver or to collect a man to come to the chapel, I stay outside and lean inwards to talk. On one occasion I do this, and inadvertently step inside. An officer comes at once and reprimands me, saying she'll have to fill in a security report on me as I've breached the regulations. The prisoner might have slammed the door shut, taken me hostage and caused tremendous problems for everyone in the prison. I must always look through the spyhole before unlocking a cell, to be sure a man isn't waiting to ambush me. It's hard to always be aware of the security of the prison, when trying to focus on the problems of the prisoner.

Visiting new prisoners can be a brief, 'Hello, you're back then?' Or perhaps a first-time offender in deep distress, then I have to sit down and listen for a long time. I feel I'm privileged to be one of the few women the men come into contact with in their largely male environment. Being older, a grandmother figure perhaps, is a positive advantage here, as I felt years before teaching in D prison that I could be a mother figure. One of my colleagues there said she felt it was vital that men had a meaningful relationship with women that wasn't sexual. For some, she felt, this might be their first experience of such a relationship.

When I first started in B prison, the shortage of chaplains meant I was often the only one in the prison and had to do all the statutory duties on my own, which could take a great deal of time, leaving me exhausted. Then the newly appointed coordinating chaplain was always willing to share these duties with me. He sometimes asked me to attend the daily governor's meeting at 8.30 am when he wasn't there. I managed to be at the prison in time for this, but found it hard, until someone suggested that, as I was a volunteer, this was not something I should be expected to do. After that, on days when the coordinating chaplain was absent, there was no chaplain at the morning meeting. It was a fairly formal affair, seldom taking more than ten minutes, and I suspect no one really noticed the absence of the chaplaincy. The heads of all the prison departments and a senior officer from each wing reported on any incidents or problems over the last 24 hours, and their plans for the next 24. Most simply said, 'Standard day, sir.' When I went I would say that there would be a silent meeting at 2.15 p.m., but I found my Quaker belief in equality prevented me from adding, 'Sir'.

Now that more chaplains have been appointed I'm almost never the only one in the prison. The chaplain who usually shares the Monday duties seems reluctant to let me do statutory duties as I'm 'only a volunteer'. I sometimes wonder if he also thinks, 'Only a Quaker.' He's usually done them all by the time I get there around nine o'clock. I miss the opportunity to meet men in this official, yet informal, way. Now I have to just 'loiter with intent', something one of the experienced chaplains advised me to do when the men are on association. Just wander around the wing, waiting for someone to come to me with some problem. This happens little at times when most men are locked up.

When they come into prison, prisoners are asked what faith they belong to. The majority say, 'None' and are entered on our lists as 'Nil'. The chaplain must check, when visiting new prisoners, that the registered faith is correct. If it's not it has to be changed, and this can only be done on an official 'Change of Religion' form in triplicate. Mistakes are frequent; I sometimes wonder if some officers enter 'Nil' as its easiest to spell.

'It's not a change, I've always been a Muslim,' is a frequent complaint.

I only met three men who had Quaker as their registered faith. I will tell Simon's story more fully in *Chapter 9*. Seamus was an Irishman who'd once slept rough on the steps of Friends House in London. 'It's a good place to sleep,' he said, 'when I'm in Hereford I go to their lunches for the homeless. I used to help set the tables out.' I lent him a copy of *Quaker Faith and Practice*, which I never saw again, but hope he made use of it. The next time he came in, however, he registered as a Roman Catholic.

Stephen registered as a Quaker because his mother was a Quaker, and he had attended Quaker meetings as a child with his grandmother. He'd never been to a meeting as an adult, and I regret that he never came to our prison meetings. Even the promise of tea and biscuits did not tempt him. I tried to visit him each time I went to the prison, and was able to let his mother know that he was coping well with his time inside, but I wasn't able to help him with this. He had a university place waiting for him when he got out.

I hope that I'll get the duties done before the men go out for their daily exercise. There are two yards for the men to walk around for an hour each day. A wing's is tiny, surrounded on all sides by the high walls of the prison. The sun only shines there at the height of summer. The yard for B and C wings is larger, with some open space around it so the men can watch the comings and goings of the prison. It's far enough from the walls for the sun to shine on a corner, which grows larger as the days lengthen, but which never covers the whole yard. In warm weather, those on 'exercise' congregate in this corner to sit and sunbathe.

'It's not real fresh air in the exercise yard,' says George.

I understand exactly what he means. Even the air in prison feels different. Walking out of the prison into sunlight, rain or fog I always feel a sense of relief, the air is fresh and free. How much more must this sense of freedom be for those walking out after being locked up for months or years? How they must really mean it when they say they'll never come back, but the odds are stacked against them: most will return. I return every Monday, week after week for some years, sometimes with a feeling of foreboding.

On the wall by the doors to the exercise yards hang a quantity of cagoules, so that prisoners can have their regulation hour of exercise whatever the weather. Few take advantage of this, and there might be no one on exercise on a really wet day. At the other extreme, exercise is popular in hot weather, with more sunbathing than exercise.

Some men choose not to go on exercise, and I hope those I've not managed to see yet are in their cells. Like many prisons, B is overcrowded, this means, for most, two men living in a cell designed for one. Sometimes, if a prisoner wants to discuss some personal problem, I have to ask his cell-mate to go outside, after checking with the officer on the wing if this is all right, or I may take the man to the chapel. Each cell is small, containing double bunks, a table and two chairs, all firmly fixed to the floor, a shelf with a television, a lavatory with wash basin and a tiny, ill-fitting, dirty, barred window too high up to see out of without climbing up. In winter it's impossible to shut this to keep out the cold; in summer it doesn't open enough to let the fresh air in. In each cell door is a spyhole, which officers can open at any time to look in.

When the practice of 'slopping out' came to an end, a lavatory and wash basin were installed in each cell. Before that prisoners had to urinate and defecate into a bucket, which was taken to the recess at the end of each landing and emptied, every morning. When I first came to the prison, staff looking through the spyhole could see men using the lavatory. Plastic, translucent curtains were later erected round them to give the men some privacy. But where else in the 21st-century would one be expected to spend 23 hours a day, and to eat all one's meals, in a lavatory, shared with a total stranger? I frequently wonder at the forbearance and lack of complaint at the almost total absence of privacy. Perhaps they've lost so much, the loss of privacy is a minor inconvenience, nevertheless, I admire their ability to rub along with their cell mates, whoever they might be. Evidence, perhaps, of the Quaker 'that of God' within each one, enabling them to survive.

When not on exercise most men can be found in their cells, few have jobs. There's one workshop where old bicycles are refurbished and sent to health workers in the Third World. This is a wonderful opportunity for a small number of men. David proudly shows me a photograph album with pictures of the bikes he's worked on, and tells me where they've gone.

'It's the first time in my life I feel I've done anything worthwhile,' he says.

Some men work in the kitchen or as cleaners. Both are privileged jobs. Cleaners are allowed out of their cells much of the day and the prison is certainly kept clean: once I saw a man cleaning the intricate Victorian wrought iron railings on a staircase with a toothbrush. At the time I was visiting a daughter in a nearby hospital, probably built around the same time, with similar stairs: the prison's staircase was far cleaner than the hospital's.

Around 11.30 a.m. men are briefly unlocked to collect their food from the kitchen; this happens twice a day, the following morning's breakfast being collected with the evening meal at around 4.30 p.m. Food is taken back to the cell to be eaten, and they are banged up until around 2 pm. C wing was built in the 20th-century, originally as a young offenders' wing. When young offenders were no longer sent to B prison, it became a drug-free wing; theoretically C category, which means the men are not locked in their cells most of the time, but free to move about the place. However, I often find them banged-up when I go there, usually because of staff shortages, which seems to be a great deal of the time, and is the reason, or excuse, for all sorts of things not happening. On C wing there is a dining room where men can eat together, and an association room. Some men still prefer to take their meals back to their cells. On C wing the cells are single occupancy, but there's no sanitation. If a man needs the lavatory at night or during times of 'lock down', which includes the lengthy lunch period, he has to ring his bell, and his door is unlocked electronically from the wing office. He can be watched on closed circuit television going to the recess.

'I'd rather use a chamber pot,' says George.

If I go out of the prison in the lunch break, I must hand in my keys, and the tally is returned. There is time now to go out and sit quietly in a side chapel in the local cathedral, letting its tranquillity wash out the stress of the previous few hours, or perhaps I take a stroll by the nearby river. I return to the prison around 2 pm, once again exchanging the tally for keys. I hand in the names of the visiting Quakers for the afternoon's meeting, and go back to the chapel to arrange the chairs round a table with *The Bible*, the book *Quaker Faith and Practice*, *Quaker Advices and Queries*, and the all important vase of flowers in the centre. Then it's time to go to the wings with lists of men who want to come. I return to the gate to meet the visitors, hoping they'll all be there in time to get back to the chapel before the men come for the meeting. We greet the men as they arrive, from the three wings, and then settle into half an hour of silence and peace. A blessed relief to all those in the chapel, followed by tea, biscuits and talk. I wonder will the men snatch at the biscuits today, so there aren't enough to go round, or will there be biscuits left on the plate at the end of the afternoon — can the depth of the silence be measured in biscuits?

Finally, I ring the wings to ask the officers to take the men back to their cells, shake hands and we make farewells all round. I take the visitors back to the gate, thanking them for making the meeting possible, and finally return to the office, deal with any phone calls that came during the meeting, write up the Day Book, and fill in the form stating how many men I've seen, how many came to the meeting. Then back to the gate again, once again to exchange keys for a tally. Going out, the outer door cannot be unlocked until everyone in this brief imprisonment has shown their tally to the operator of the doors behind his glass screen, to demonstrate that all keys are safely back in the cupboard labelled, 'To be kept locked at all times.' It seldom is as keys are continually being issued and returned

Once a month all the chaplains meet to discuss the business of the chaplaincy, and its inevitable problems. An officer from prison security often comes to these meetings to ensure we're aware of the vital importance of security. One rule in particular frequently causes problems: staff who meet a man in prison are not allowed to have contact with him once he's released; a restriction that causes frustration to those on both sides of the door

'That's impossible,' says a Catholic chaplain, 'I'm a parish priest and ex-inmates often come to mass.'

'That's all right in the church,' says the security officer, 'but you mustn't invite them home for a coffee.'

'But my home is attached to the church, that's where we serve coffee after mass.'

'How many doors between the church and the room where you serve coffee?'

'One.'

'That's all right. It's still part of the church. If there were two it would have been your home.'

Relationships saved by a door?

Contact with those who've been moved to another prison is also forbidden, without permission from the governor. On one occasion a chaplain sent a postcard from her holiday to a prisoner who'd been moved to another prison. He replied, care of the chaplaincy, and his letter was intercepted.

'What do you think you can do for this man that the chaplains in the prison where he is now can't?' the governor asked her when she was summoned to appear before him, 'you could be dismissed if this happens again.'

These restrictions on relationships are some of the more frustrating parts of work in a prison chaplaincy. It appears not only common sense but common humanity to allow a relationship to come to its natural conclusion, not be ended in this abrupt and arbitrary way. Surely this will have to change, if we are to see those leaving prison stay out. The prison drug service is called CARAT—Counselling, Assessment, Referral, Advice and Throughcare. The last of these is described as 'providing post-release follow-up of inmates for a maximum of eight weeks.' I don't know if this follow-up means being followed by those whom the prisoner knows from prison. I suspect not, as each man has two probation officers, one inside and one outside the prison. Surely maintaining contact with someone one knows might work better? 'Through the gate' is a common phrase, used in government publications concerning 'reducing reoffending'. Do they realise that once someone goes through the gate, that's the end of all contact? I have known chaplains lose their jobs because they did not abide by this.

In one case a most experienced chaplain, who'd had a special relationship with many men, who all seemed to know and love him, had been there so long he'd met many of their fathers in this prison before they were born. Years ago, a governor asked him to help a particular man after he was released. He continued, with the prison governor's approval, to do this for many years, with a succession of men, through a succession of governors. Then a new governor decided he was breaking the rules and he was dismissed, after years of service, with not even a chance to say goodbye to his colleagues, let alone to apologise to the men who were expecting to come to his Bible study class that evening. We were told to say, if asked about him, that he'd retired. Although he was coming up to retirement age, this was not believed.

'You don't organize Bible study for the day you're going to retire,' said Don.

Another frustration of prison work is the fact that, paid or unpaid, a chaplain works for the Prison Service, thus you can't offer the confidentiality you would outside. I nearly gave up my job once, rather than tell an officer the identity of a man who had complained about being bullied.

'You work for the Prison Service,' I was told. Reluctantly I went to tell the man that I would have to break my promise that what he said was between the two of us. Unconcerned, he said, 'Not to worry. I decided I'd better tell the officer.' One can't expect gratitude from those in prison, though one very frequently gets it.

While attitudes to prisoners have changed dramatically since B prison was built, with officers now seeing themselves in a caring as much as a custodial role, nevertheless an atmosphere of Victorian horror seems to me to hang in the air of the prison. Despite changing attitudes and improved conditions, 21st-century officers and prisoners breath the Victorian certainty exuded by those thick walls, built to last. Echoes of earlier brutality can almost be heard on its landings. The buildings have witnessed so much suffering, so many wasted lives in their 200-year history. Men were hanged here in the past, do their ghosts haunt men locked up here today? It would be easy to believe they do.

Yet somehow, those in B prison manage to overcome the historical and architectural gloom. Relationships between officers and prisoners are relaxed and friendly.

'It's the best prison I've been in,' says Ben, 'and I've been in a few.'

George agrees, 'I know there's always an officer I can go to if I need to talk.'

'Many of them here seem to care,' says Ben.

CHAPTER TWO

Faith in Prison

'HM Prison Service Chaplaincy is committed to serving the needs of prisoners, staff and religious traditions by engaging all human experience. We will work collaboratively, respecting the integrity of each tradition and discipline.

We believe that faith and the search for meaning directs and inspires life, and are committed to providing sacred spaces and dedicated teams to deepen and enrich human experience. By celebrating the goodness of life and exploring the human condition we aim to cultivate in each individual a responsibility for contributing to the common good. We will contribute to the care of prisoners to enable them to lead law-abiding and useful lives in custody and after release.'

Statement of Purpose agreed by the Prison Chaplaincy Council
and the Chaplaincy Senior Management Team, 2003

Chaplains have always played an important part in prisons. As places to be sent as a punishment, as opposed to awaiting punishment, prisons date back only to the late-18th century. Before that offenders were transported to the colonies. Before that public humiliation in the stocks or branding were common; death was the penalty for very many offences.

The 19th-century which saw the end of transportation and the number of capital offences reduced, was the heyday of prison building. The Victorians were great prison builders, and also great believers in the power of Christianity for social control. Wrongdoers were seen as having souls that could be saved, so the chapel was central to Victorian prisons. A healthy dose of Christianity, with hard work, would, it was thought, transform criminals into the industrious workers needed by the new manufacturing society. In a phrase popular today, they believed that only Christianity could enable them to 'turn their lives around.'

In those days prisoners were often kept in solitary confinement for most of the time, with only the crank to turn all day for company; it was hoped they would reflect on their crime and repent. They were even forbidden to speak when with their fellow inmates. During exercise they might wear a hood, so they couldn't see the others. You can still see in Lincoln Castle Museum the old prison chapel, with high sided pews designed so that each member of the congregation couldn't see anyone apart from the chaplain. It's not surprising that in his *Ballad of Reading Gaol* Oscar Wilde wrote:

'Some grow mad, and all grow bad,
And none a word may say.'

While today few think that Christianity, or even religion, is the only way to turn one's life around, chaplains still play an important part in the work of prisons. Prison chaplaincies are groups of chaplains working together for the good of the prison inmates and staff. All chaplains are theoretically of equal status, with a coordinating chaplain appointed to organize the work. Some are volunteers, as I was, others paid by the Ministry of Justice who lay down the 'statutory duties' to be performed each day.

Originally, all prison chapels were Church of England. In the mid-20th-century they became ecumenical, by the early-21st they were multi-faith, reflecting the multicultural nature of modern society. Today prison chaplains represent all the major faiths, including Pagans. When I was a chaplain the main omission was the Rastafarians. I gathered that the prison chaplaincy council wanted to include these, and many coming into prison when asked for their faith say, 'Rastafarian.' The Ministry of Justice, however, did not permit this as a registered faith, I suspect because some Rastafarians say smoking cannabis is part of it. But Rastafarians I met said this isn't actually so. At a prison chaplains' conference I once met two Rastafarians, I recognised them by their green, red and yellow hats. I went over to say how surprised I was to see them.

'We're actually probation officers,' one of them said, 'but we work as part of the chaplaincy team, because there are so many Rastafarians in our prison, and our coordinating chaplain thinks we can help them.'

This has changed since I retired. The ban on Rastafarians being able to practice their faith was found to be in breach of the 2010 equality legislation, and Rastafarianism is now permitted in prisons.

As long as they are registered as belonging to a faith acknowledged by the Ministry of Justice, prisoners have the right of access to a chaplain of that faith, attendance at services, and religious artefacts necessary for the faith. Chaplains of all faiths cooperate in the pastoral care of all those in prison, of any faith or none. In B prison festivals of all major faiths were celebrated, with the kitchen providing Chinese food for the Chinese New Year, as well as mince pies at Christmas.

I have learned that many prisons have rabbis who come into prison on a regular basis, often as part of the chaplaincy team and particularly in London and larger cities. They meet with the Jewish inmates, including on occasions such as Rosh Hashanah and Yom Kippur, to conduct services and share hallowed meals. In the time I was a chaplain we only ever had one man at B prison who registered as a Jew. A rabbi came all the way from London to see him. It turned out the prisoner had said he was a Jew because someone had told him that Jews get kosher food and thought this sounded like a good idea! He (the rabbi) said in his experience people may not say they are Jews when they get sent to prison, as they would prefer the rabbi not to know this.

The different faiths have so much in common. Buddhist prison chaplains must all belong to an organization called, 'Angulimala' after a notoriously violent man, a serial killer who wanted to collect 1,000 human little fingers, which he wore as a necklace. When he had 999 he saw the Buddha walking in the forest. He tried to overtake him, but although the Buddha was walking slowly, leisurely, he couldn't catch up.

'Stop!' he shouted to Buddha.

'I have stopped. I have stopped killing and harming. It's time for you also to stop,' said Buddha.

Angulimala was so impressed that he threw away his weapons and followed Buddha, becoming a monk.

Muslims say, 'Allah, most high says: "He who approaches near to me one span, I will approach to him one cubit; and he who approaches near to me one cubit, I will approach him one fathom; and who ever approaches me walking, I will come to him running, and he who meets me with sins equivalent to the whole world, I will greet him with forgiveness equal to it."'

Christians have the story of the prodigal son. However, society is unforgiving.

All those working in prisons are expected to respect diversity. The official Prison Service definition of 'diversity' is

'the mosaic of people who bring a variety of backgrounds, styles, perspectives, values and beliefs as assets to the groups and organizations with which they interact.'

This sounds similar to *Quaker Advice* No. 22 to:

'Respect the wide diversity among us in our lives and relationships. Refrain from making prejudiced judgements about the life journey of others. Do you foster the spirit of mutual understanding and forgiveness which our discipleship asks of us? Remember that each one of us is unique, precious, a child of God.'

Quakers have a long, proud history of imprisonment for conscience's sake from their early days of refusing to accept the laws of the 17th-century to their imprisonment as pacifists in two world wars, and later as peace protestors. On release, conscientious objectors imprisoned in the First World War campaigned against some of the brutalities of our prisons, including the silence rule, ironic from a group which sees God in silence.

Throughout their history, the belief in 'that of God in all' has led Quakers to work for prison reform, as well as to work for peace. In the 1680s William Penn, Quaker founder of Pennsylvania, was insisting on rehabilitation, saying that prisoners should be helped to learn a trade so that they could make an honest living when released. In the 19th-century Elizabeth Fry visited the women and children in Newgate Prison, London, and agitated tirelessly for prison reform, not always with the support of her local meeting. Today Quakers can be found supporting the Howard League for Penal Reform, the Prison Reform Trust, working in restorative justice (see *Chapter 10*) and the Alternatives to Violence Project in prisons. Quakers were much involved in setting up Circles of Support and Accountability, working with released sex offenders, to ensure they do not to re-offend. Our *Quaker Advices and Queries* No. 33 includes the words:

'Bear witness to the humanity of all people, including those who break society's conventions or its laws ... Are you working to bring about a just and compassionate society which allows everyone to develop their capacities and fosters a desire to serve.'

It is not surprising that Quakers welcome the opportunity for QPCs to bring some Quaker ethos into prisons, despite fears by some that they are too close to those with keys, rather than identifying with the locked-up and vulnerable. It can be hard to embrace both roles.

Today, the majority of prisons have a Quaker chaplain, who works with chaplains of other faiths 'celebrating the goodness of life and exploring the human condition ... contributing to the common good.' Some organize Quaker meetings, others work in different ways answering that of God in all. I organized a silent, but not specifically Quaker, meeting (see next chapter). Quaker meetings are surprisingly popular in prisons; from the journals of early Quakers we know that they were held in the 18th-century.

B prison's original chapel was an imposing space, between A and B wings. Lofty, with high church windows, it was extremely cold in winter. It felt like a non-conformist chapel rather than a church; with its galleries it was large enough to hold the whole prison population at the time it was built. The atmosphere of 19th-century hell-fire seemed to hang in the air of that great space, yet here 21st-century chaplains offered solace, sympathy or support at times of need. When the roof started to leak, as happens with church roofs, the chaplaincy was allocated a disused workshop as a 'temporary' chapel. Temporary became permanent as the prison authorities found a better use for the refurbished old chapel. In many ways I preferred the converted workshop, its atmosphere was less full of hell-fire, there was more light and it was possible to heat it, although the heater made a great deal of noise, disturbing our silent meetings. But the old chapel had the advantage of being central to the prison, easy to take a man there for a quiet chat. Going to the new chapel involved a long walk, with many doors to lock and unlock as you went, with perhaps an unhappy prisoner becoming more and more distressed as you went along.

Both the old and the new chapels were the only place large enough for a staff meeting. The old chapel was adapted to its new use and thus became unsuitable for a large meeting; so the new chapel was still frequently commandeered for this purpose, and any chaplaincy activities that had been planned for that time had to be cancelled or postponed, often at short notice. This was a continual reminder that we worked in and for a prison: the main purpose of the entire building, even the chapel, supposed to be a 'sacred space', was subordinate to that purpose.

When I first became a QPC, my Quaker faith was very much that of a Universalist Quaker: I tended not to call myself a Christian, and believed all faiths to be equally valid; I was slightly uneasy about the use of the word God, preferring to speak of the Inner Light or Spirit. Thus I was pleased to find that the chaplaincy was 'multi-faith'. Chaplains are specifically forbidden to proselytise, but all can share our vision of our own particular faith. William Noblett was Chaplain General in 2003, when this was accepted by the Chaplaincy Council, and the words at the start of this chapter were agreed. 'Celebrating the goodness of life and exploring the human condition ... finding meaning' made sense to me, something I was happy to cooperate with.

I was, however, somewhat disturbed to find that some chaplains in B prison weren't happy with becoming multi-faith. I heard some harsh words about Noblett, some bordering on Islamophobia. Some seemed to think he was somehow belittling Christianity to placate Muslims. This about a man who has written a most moving, and very Christian book, *Prayers for People in Prison*.

'We have two imams for a dozen or so Muslims. There are far more Christians per chaplain for us' said one of the Christian chaplains. He ignored the fact that both imams were part-time, one only coming in for Friday prayers. He seemed unhappy at the care taken to provide a Thermos flask for Muslims during Ramadan, so that they had a hot meal after sunset. Some chaplains seemed to look on other faiths as a threat to their own, rather than an opportunity for enrichment and mutual nourishment. Beckford and Gilliat's *Religion in Prison: Equal Rites in a Multi-faith Society* shows how hard it was for Anglican chaplains to relinquish control of religion in prisons, and become what they call 'facilitators' and 'brokers'. They write of major tensions resulting from the change. I witnessed this tension in B prison, arriving around the time it officially became multi-faith.

When I first joined the team there was no coordinating chaplain, the acting coordinator was an Evangelical Methodist. He'd spent his working life in B prison, seemed to know all the men by name, had known many of their fathers and was deeply respected by both staff and prisoners; I couldn't but admire his faith.

'I respect Quakers,' he said to me, 'but tell me—where does the Inner Light come from?'

'I think I need notice of that question,' I replied.

The next time I was in the prison I said, 'I think it comes from the Big Bang.' He was horrified. 'Oh, no. It can only come from Christ.'

When a coordinating chaplain was eventually appointed, he turned out to be even more evangelical. I once heard him say to a visitor, 'Only Christ can turn the lives of some of these men around.' Was this the 19th-century chapel speaking through a 21st-century chaplain?

'I'm sorry, I can't agree,' I had to interrupt, 'I think this happens in very many ways. There are so many books written by those who found salvation in the arts, writing, restorative justice, education. It's just a case of finding another way to be. They usually meet someone in prison who believes in them, can see their potential, often for the first time in their lives.'

The coordinating chaplain couldn't agree. After a few years this coordinator left to be replaced by the imam, and multi-faith became a reality in our chaplaincy.

In my first few months in B prison there was a shortage of chaplains, so I was occasionally asked if I would come to the Sunday Service, to host a visiting church, who would be taking it. This involved meeting them at the gate, unlocking doors for them, and liaising with the officers bringing men to the chapel. One Evangelical church, came in regularly, and was popular with the men; I found its ways somewhat disturbing. They had many lovely long-haired young women who sang solos beautifully, and the men would applaud vigorously at the end, as they did when one of the prisoners read a lesson. The words of hymns for the congregation to sing, usually called 'songs' were displayed on a large screen from an overhead projector and were simple. One went:

'God gotta hold of my life, and He won't let me go.'

These few words were sung over and over again, with the men becoming more and more emotional. If the congregation were invited to come forward and accept Christ as their saviour, there was no shortage of volunteers. It felt, to me, that this was almost abuse of men in a particularly vulnerable situation. Yet they obviously enjoyed these services, they came in large numbers, and participated fully. They were offered hope at a time when life might feel hopeless.

I was glad when more chaplains were appointed so I was no longer asked to come to Sunday Services. Yet the longer I spent in the prison the more I found that I could respect this form of Christianity, as I was able to respect other faiths. While I found, and still find, the notion of being 'saved' superficial and questionable, Evangelical churches often seem to be involved in truly Christian work that could put Quakers to shame. This includes the Sycamore Tree Restorative Justice Programme, and Angle Tree which provides Christmas presents for the children of those in prison. I began to be able to say 'Yes,' when asked if I was a Christian, though this would be on my own definition, which did not include belief in the resurrection, or that the Christian God is the only God.

Another QPC said that when asked by a prisoner if he believed that Jesus was the son of God, he replied, 'Yes. And so are you.' I hope I would have said the same had I been asked that question, but I don't remember ever being asked that.

Gradually I started to use the word God more easily, and to be able to respond to men's requests for prayers. By the time I retired, I realised just how much I had gained from being a QPC, far more than I was able to offer. At the same time my Universalist faith was wider and deeper, I was more able to be 'open to new Light', in the words of *Quaker Advices and Queries,* whether this came from those with keys or without them.

One of the many things I failed to do in the prison was to introduce Prison Phoenix Trust yoga and meditation classes, which are surprisingly popular in the many prisons. Our chaplaincy said they couldn't afford it—it would have involved two paid hours of a tutor's time at around £20 an hour once a week. I asked the learning and skills department if they could offer it, but they said they could only provide it if requested by another department of the prison. I told CARATS, the drugs team, about it who said it sounded worthwhile, but they were offering their own form of meditation. I never found a way to get the Phoenix Trust accepted; I should have persisted.

The Phoenix Trust isn't attached to any particular faith, but covers all. I told men about it because as well as running classes they publish free books and CDs to help prisoners with yoga and meditation. Once they send away for these, prisoners get a regular newsletter sent to the prison. The trust sent these to me, and I would take them to the prisoner concerned. They also sent a form asking if any prisoner they were in contact with had been released or moved to another prison; then the newsletter would go there. Thus I met many men who had been in contact with Phoenix in previous prisons, which was frequently the opportunity for an interesting chat, possibly swelling the numbers at our silent meetings. Many had been meditating for years.

This was how I met Frank, who'd learned yoga in a previous prison. For a few weeks, while he was with us, he led a 15 minute yoga session after the silence of our meetings. Everyone joined in, and we all appreciated it.

'Meditation's a real help to me,' said Frank, 'it gives me a reason to get out of bed. It gets me out of my head.'

Peter Pringle, in his book *About Time*, writes of how yoga and meditation helped him to get through a life sentence (which was originally a death sentence, for a crime of which he was finally acquitted, after 15 years):

> '...I stretched out on the floor just to let go, not making conscious effort. And I arrived in the meditative state of being. It was like magic! Afterwards I felt calm, rested and very clear-headed. That's when I began to understand what was meant by "do without dong", "concentrate without concentrating." My yoga efforts also improved and my anger became much less. I was able to study. It was like a miracle to me.' (p.170)

The popularity of yoga and meditation shouldn't have surprised me. The proportion of the prison population who attend chapel in prison is much higher than the churchgoing of the general population. Many say they are 'prison chapel goers', others go simply to get out of their cells. But even some of these are converted to one of the faiths, and there are many books by such people, the most famous being Jonathan Aitken's *Pride and Perjury*. Many of them tell of their road from gangster or drug-dealer to Christian, and are popular with prisoners, particularly when there is plenty of the gangster days for them to identify with.

Bible study was also popular as an evening class, until evening activities ceased, victims of the cuts. I was impressed by the knowledge some men had of *The Bible*. If, in one of our discussions, I said I wasn't sure where a particular story in *The Bible* came from, there always seemed to be someone who could find out quite quickly.

I found, rather to my surprise, that everyone seemed to know the words of the Lord's Prayer. Was this from school assemblies, or prison chapel services? Will this continue in the future, now that school assemblies, except in church schools, no longer seem to involve prayer? I learned that Catholics don't say, 'For thine is the kingdom, the power and the glory, for ever and ever.'

'We don't say that,' said Carl, the new Catholic.

'Why don't you?' asked Spenser.

'I don't know,' said Carl.

I had to find a Catholic chaplain for an answer. It seems, apparently, that the different denominations take the words from different gospels, which vary slightly.

'There must be a God, because everyone prays in the dock,' said Carl . The group agreed.

'Not always the same God,' said Spenser. Again there was agreement.

Men often read passages of *The Bible* in the silent meetings. I wondered sometimes about the popularity of the *Book of Revelation*, particularly the more bloodthirsty sections.

'Then the seven angels that held the seven trumpets prepared to blow them.

The first blew his trumpet; and there came hail and fire mingled with blood, and this was hurled upon the earth. A third of the earth was burnt, a third of the trees were burnt, all the green grass was burnt.

The second angel blew his trumpet; and what looked like a great blazing mountain was hurled into the sea. A third of the sea was turned to blood, a third of the living creatures in it died, and a third of the ships on it foundered.

The third angel blew his trumpet; and a great star shot from the sky, flaming like a torch; and it fell on a third of the rivers and springs. The name of the star was Wormwood; and a third of the water turned to wormwood, and men in great numbers died of the water because it had been poisoned.' (*Revelation*, Chapter 8)

'I do wonder what Revelation is doing in *The Bible*,' said a Catholic deaconess I met at a chaplaincy conference, 'Christianity would be very different if they'd included the *Gospel of Mary Magdalene* rather than *Revelation*.' She'd joined me in the room set aside for silent prayer, in the worship time of the conference. I was the only one using it and was glad of her company.

'These Christians are too noisy for me,' she said, coming to the quiet with relief from the enthusiastic evangelical singing we could hear in the distance.

When I was first in B prison the Prison Service offered new chaplains a course called 'Starting Out'. This was largely a correspondence course, ending with two days at the Prison Service College at Newbold Revel in Warwickshire. It was an excellent introduction to chaplaincy work; part of it involved talking to various people in the prison about how they saw the chaplaincy, which I found a good way of finding out how we fitted into the life of the prison. We were also required to write an article for a fictitious parish magazine. I called mine 'Eggshells and Knife Edges'. Extracts read:

'Interviewing prison staff, prisoners and chaplains was part of the training I have just completed, as a recently appointed Quaker Prison Minister in a typically overcrowded, understaffed, 'Victorian' (built 1792) local prison. I was pleasantly surprised to find the chaplaincy, the chapel and the chaplains held in high esteem by those I spoke to.'

'A prison officer told me that chapel is the only place where it is "safe to cry", so breaking bad news to prisoners is a task for a chaplain.'

'A prisoner said, "He gave me new life … I hung myself when I was at my lowest ebb … the chaplain brought me back".'

'A chaplain said that what prisoners most need from chaplains is "acceptance"—whatever they have done, whatever the chaplain may feel, that person must be accepted and seen as someone valued in the sight of God. No one is outside the knowledge and love of God.'

'At a typical Sunday morning service in the chapel, as well as those who have come to get out of their cells and have a laugh with friends from other wings, are the deeply devout. I shall never forget the unaccompanied solo singing of "There is a Green Hill Far Away", to the tune of "There is a House in New Orleans" on Good Friday, or the quiet sincerity of the Maundy Thursday service, where Catholic and Anglican chaplains washed and dried prisoners' feet together.'

'The prison chapel may be the only place in the prison with a sense of space, of calm, of something beyond everyday horrors. More than one person told me they felt better by just going into the chapel. It can be a 'sacred space.'

'Going to prison is a traumatic experience, and may be a turning point in many lives. For some it is the start of a lifetime of increasingly lengthy sentences: others may turn to religion for convenience, as we do for baptisms, marriages and funerals. For some of these this may result in conversion to a faith that makes this sentence their last. Others may not come to church again until they are next in prison: "I usually come to chapel when I'm inside, but I haven't this time", one told me.'

The last full week in November sees Prisons Week. This started in 1975. Organized by a committee of prison chaplains and other Christians involved in work with prisoners and their families, its aim is to encourage prayer in churches and the wider Christian community for the needs of prisoners.

Roman Catholic chaplains used to bring in boxes full of them for free distribution. Everyone wanted a rosary.

'Can I have a blue one please? I've got a yellow one,' said Spenser.

At one time I, a Quaker, used to carry a rosary round in my pocket to
save myself the trouble of going back to the chapel each time I was asked
for one. When that chaplain left the supply ran out, and his successor didn't
continue the practice. I'm not sure if this was because the previous chaplain
had been funding this out of his own pocket, or because of a story I heard
more than once, repeated at a chaplaincy meeting: if a drug-dealer had
drugs to sell he wore his rosary outside his sweatshirt, if he had no supplies
he would keep it hidden. I suspect this is a prison myth. Certainly rosaries
seemed popular, but now men have to buy them through the canteen (the
prison shop), like other religious requirements, prayer mats, incense sticks,
etc. It was simple to deal with 'rosemary' requests after this. I believe the
rosaries were a special prison design, the string too weak to be used as a liga-
ture, again I don't know if this is fact or myth.

Requests for prayer were harder to deal with. The belief in that of God in
everyone makes intercessory prayer problematic for a Quaker. The first time
I heard this request was in my early days as a chaplain, before I was issued
with keys. I was going round with a Free Church chaplain, who would take
me to visit men who he thought needed a visit, and a chance to talk.

'I'm in court tomorrow, can you say a prayer for me?' Tony asked.

'I'm not sure I can,' I said, 'but the senior chaplain will when he gets back'.

When he did, Tony asked again. We all bowed our heads, as the chaplain
produced the desired words, 'Heavenly Father…in your mercy…we beseech
thee…'. He ended by praying, 'May justice be done.' I thought I saw a look
on Tony's face that said he didn't want justice, he wanted an acquittal. 'I
never pray for them to get off,' the chaplain later explained, 'but I do know
that's what they want'.

I took my problem with prayer to an experienced QPC, who gave me excellent advice. She told me she always explained that Quakers pray in silence,
but if the man would share a few moments silence with her, words would
come. This worked for her, and seemed to work for me. When I was asked for
a prayer for someone else, I usually said, 'Tell me a bit about them.' If it was
for themselves I asked about the problem. After a chat and a silence, words

did appear from somewhere. I often said something on the lines of 'May you become aware of that of God within you. May you find comfort in this.' Or 'May your girlfriend realise that there is that of God in her, which will help her to cope.' When asked for prayer for a court appearance, I might say, 'May that of God within you support you. May the judge recognise your Inner Light.'

Sometimes, as the phrase became more common among Quakers, I would talk of 'Holding in the Light'. Occasionally, when I felt this was wanted I would end, 'For Jesus' sake.' I never felt comfortable with this or knew if it was wanted, but men were usually grateful for my efforts, whatever we said, and often thanked me unnecessarily fulsomely for my apparent intercession with the Almighty.

'I feel "all warm" inside,' said Jason, after some silence and prayer for his girlfriend who had had an abortion.

Sometimes the man himself said a prayer. Sometimes we said The Lord's Prayer together. I found it a useful form of words to use on occasion; I remember reciting it through the spyhole with Mark in solitary confinement; the officer said it was not safe to unlock him, as he had a problem with women. 'I want to see the Catholic,' he would object when he saw me.

'He's not in today.' The Lord's Prayer was the next best thing as far as Mark was concerned. I was glad Carl had taught me not to say 'For thine is the Kingdom, the power and the glory.'

The officer stood over me throughout. Perhaps he didn't trust me not to go in; silence seemed impossible in the situation.

Blessings proved more difficult. As a Quaker, I can't believe in a God who'd bestow a blessing because I asked for it. One day a total stranger asked, 'Can you say a blessing for me.'

I said, 'I don't feel qualified to bless you, but I'll ask a chaplain who is to come and see you.'

'Oh don't bother then.'

I worried about this for some time, and then started using Celtic blessings:

May the road rise up to meet you,
May the wind be always at your back.
May the sun shine on warm upon your face,
The rains fall soft upon your fields.

And, until we meet again, may you be held in the palm of God's hand.

I explained that these were ancient Celtic words, but felt that the rather too rural images were often inappropriate. For very troubled men I might use:

Deep peace of the running wave to you
Deep peace of the flowing air to you
Deep peace of the quiet earth to you
Deep peace of the shining stars to you
Deep peace of the gentle night to you
Moon and stars pour their healing light on you
Deep peace of Christ.

I used these for a time, then, on the holy island of Iona, I had an amazing experience at a creative writing retreat, led by the poet Roselle Anguin, entitled 'Islands of the Heart'. It had nothing to do with the abbey, although its presence seemed to infuse it. It had nothing to do with Quakers, but we started each day with an hour of silence, which felt to me very like a Quaker meeting. We could use the silence to think, to meditate, to write. Most spent at least part of the time writing. I remember sitting quietly, listening to the scratch of pens, the rustle of paper, hearing in these creative sounds the spirit at work.

On the first evening we shared a silence where I had such a strong sense that this was a Quaker meeting that, afterwards, I turned to the person next to me and asked, 'Are you a Quaker?'

'Yes, are you?' she said, 'I saw you on Glasgow station and was sure you were coming here, but not quite sure enough then to ask.'

These silences on Iona were powerful. One morning, out of that silence, the words of a Quaker blessing came to me; I wrote them down, and after that, every time I was asked for a blessing, I used them, explaining that this was a Quaker blessing. Sometimes I saw men crossing themselves as I recited

Dear child of God, you are blessed.
God within you blesses you from within.
Allow yourself to accept this blessing,
May you find the peace you seek.

CHAPTER THREE

Seeking 'A Gathered Stillness'

'The mood and temper of the public in regard to the treatment of crime and criminals is one of the most unfailing tests of the civilisation of any country…There is a treasure, if only you can find it, in the heart of every person.'

Winston Churchill speaking in the House of Commons on 20 July 1910

I never thought of Winston Churchill as a Quaker, yet the 'treasure … in the heart of every person' sounds remarkably like the Quaker 'that of God in all'. When I accepted my area meeting's nomination to be the Quaker chaplain in my local prison, I didn't think I'd be organizing silent meetings. I shared what I think is a common misunderstanding that Quaker silence is something very middle-class, requiring certain levels of education, intelligence and understanding. How wrong I was. Our advice to come to meetings for worship with 'heart and mind prepared' implies that something cerebral may go on: this is not essential. Silence is classless.

I soon discovered that those with little education, who were perhaps not used to using their minds much, appreciate silence no less than seasoned Quakers. They didn't need to understand Quaker theology, or to read a leaflet on what to expect. When I first started, before I realised this, I offered a weekly evening discussion group, and invited local Friends to come and join us. We always ended with about five minutes silence, which was sometimes spoiled by giggles, but was more often profound; some of those coming remarked on it. Around a dozen men came, but it was obvious that many were there just to get out of their cells: if a wing had association that evening, numbers from that wing dropped.

When the prison ended evening activities as an economy measure, discussions moved to afternoons. Numbers went down to two or three, and discussions deteriorated, largely, I suspect, because no-one on education could come.

'I really like the silence,' said Sam one week. So I decided to change the shape of the meetings, and to risk a silent meeting, followed by discussion. This was probably the best thing I did in my time in the prison.

I thought that a 'Quaker Meeting' would mean little to those who might come, who might vaguely think of porridge oats. With help from local Friends I worded a notice which I put on every wing saying:

MULTI-FAITH
SILENT MEETING for MEDITATION,
MINDFULNESS, PRAYER, WORSHIP

This is open to anyone of any faith or none, who would like to share about half an hour's silence.

Silence is in short supply in prison, but many find it very precious. It can be healing. Silence lies at the heart of many religious faiths, and is deep within each of us. For some that deep place is God, or where we can meet our God. Others find that we leave a silence refreshed, renewed, healed.

Meeting with others in silence can be even more powerful. We support one another, as we share our silence, and feel the good within us strengthened. We remain alert and open to the silence, to the spirit, to each other, to our God.

Quakers base their worship on silence. A group of Quakers comes into the prison on Mondays to give you the chance to join us in a time of silence. At the end there will be a time for discussion.

You will be very welcome, do come.

Few came because they read these notices. The chaplain taking the Sunday Service would advertise the meeting, and men could sign up on a list in the chapel. I used to invite any Buddhists or Hindus among our inmates, particularly when there was no chaplain of their faith at the time (something that happened frequently); a few Pagans came from time to time; occasionally a Muslim, taking his biscuits and tea bag to be consumed later during Ramadan; sometimes Rastafarians. For a few weeks a group of Roman Catholic travellers, who had all been arrested together in a van loaded with stolen lead joined us. They were busy with their rosaries in the silence, and assured us that they never took lead from church roofs. However, most of those who came registered their religion as 'Nil'; they came for the silence.

When I first started these meetings, officers on the wings were frequently sceptical when they saw the list of those who had signed up to come:

'What him? Sit in silence?'

'He's asked to come. To try.'

After a few years they were less surprised, but usually referred to it as 'silent prayer.'

Every week I gave my lists to the officers on each wing, with a request that those men be brought to the chapel at 2.15 p.m. Most weeks I had to ring at least one wing, to ask where the men were. Sometimes an officer would say, 'X is on education, Y has a doctor's appointment, the others said they'd changed their minds and didn't want to come after all.' I was never too sure about the last of these.

I decided to collect the men myself, which I did for some years. The wing staff seemed happy with this. I'd go to C wing first, pick up the men on the list, move on to B wing, finally collecting A wing men and escorting them all to the chapel. This meant the men from C wing visited the other two wings, which was not allowed, and I often lost men temporarily, particularly Spenser, as they went to shout through doors to their friends and relations on other wings. Spenser had many friends.

Eventually I was told this was a breach of security, and could lead to fights, so I had to go back to the approved system, with all its frustrations. Sometimes we had to wait for up to half an hour for all the men to come. Then, before we could start I had to ring Communications to tell them how many men are in the chapel.

Gradually our numbers grew, partly thanks to Simon, our registered Quaker; we often had more than 20 names on the list, but education, legal visits and doctors' appointments reduced numbers to around ten, with two visiting Quakers. We almost never had the same group two weeks running; few meetings did not contain at least one for whom this was a new experience. Those who came appreciated the silence, which was usually deep.

'It's so quiet in here. This is the only place in the prison we can get away from all the noise, the banging and shouting,' said Sam.

Others agreed, and visiting Friends often said the meetings were truly 'gathered', to use a Quaker phrase. I felt there was a quality to our meetings based on a shared suffering and despair, which is not often found in Quaker meeting houses today.

I was blessed with a small group of Friends from the area meeting who came regularly to share these meetings in prison. Such a group was essential if the meeting was to be anything like a meeting for worship: I couldn't be the only Quaker present, in a group most of whom would know very little, if anything about Quakerism. Most Friends visited us about once a month. This group became more and more important to me over the years. Very few left it, though some moved away and others came to take their places. We would all gather together once, or perhaps twice, a year outside the prison for a meeting for worship, discussion of the prison meeting and its attenders, followed by a shared lunch. Over the years the group started to feel like a meeting for worship with its own personality, distinct from the meetings to which we each belonged. I came to feel the very real support of these Friends; they in turn all said how much they gained from coming to meetings in B prison. I'm sure the prison meetings met a need in the prisoners who came, due in part to those who joined in from local meetings, bringing their diverse concerns and interests. Those who came from inside were able to meet a group of people very different in important ways from those they would normally meet.

As in all Quaker meetings our silence was followed by a cup of tea, biscuits and discussion. This caused problems. At first I would bring in the refreshments with me.

'That could be considered to be "trafficking", it could lose you your job. You know the rule — "nothing in, nothing out",' said the coordinating chaplain. This was made clear at the training, but somehow I'd thought these refreshments didn't count. So I went to the kitchen and begged, and for a time they supplied us with refreshments.

'I can't go on giving you biscuits,' said the friendly kitchen officer, 'you need to requisition them.'

So I had to convince the governor in change of the chapel that tea and biscuits are essential to a Quaker meeting. When I finally got her agreement, which took some months, I went to supplies with the necessary form. The officer there said,

> 'You can have coffee, long life milk and biscuits through the kitchen, but the tea and sugar will have to come from another source where they're cheaper, but you'll have to wait until another department orders something, as there's a minimum order of £50.'

So for some time I was running between the kitchen and stores chasing after refreshments for the meetings.

The discussions after the silence gave me and visiting Friends glimpses into the lives of those whom we might not normally expect to meet: here we met as equals. Our testimony to equality took on a new meaning as we shared the silence.

'I really like us sitting in a circle,' Hugh frequently said to newcomers. 'It shows we're all equal here.'

It was only later, when I read my prison diary (see *Chapter 4*), that I realised we were still essentially very different. Our equality with the prisoners only went so far.

In these discussions men might share terrible problems, others would offer sympathy, support and suggestions. They had been there. They understood. They could help each other far more than we visitors could help them. I was frequently reminded of the words of the 17th-century Quaker Isaac Pennington, imprisoned six times for his Quaker beliefs. He wrote,

> 'Our life is love, and peace, and tenderness; and bearing one with another, and not laying accusations one against another; but praying for one another, and helping one another up with a tender hand.'
>
> *Quaker Faith and Practice.*

Sometimes our discussions centred on faith, or what we mean by God. 'What do Pagans believe?' asked Sam.

'We believe in the unity of all life. We respect nature. People should be free to do what they like, as long as they don't hurt anyone else. We should help each other,' said Jason.

'Do you believe in God?'

'Yes, but also the Goddess.'

Quakers present agreed that this sounded remarkably similar to Quakerism.

'But I'm a Druid,' said Jason, 'don't call me a Pagan. People don't like Pagans. They think we're evil in some way. We're not.'

'That's because the early Christians wanted to convert the Pagans, they told lies about them to make people convert to Christianity. There were Pagans long before there were Christians,' said Simon.

'Yes, we're the oldest religion,' said Jason. 'The Christians were really cruel, burning witches. Saying they were evil, when really they were using spells to cure people before there were medicines.'

'Like the Crusaders,' said Spencer, 'killing those of another faith.'

Similarly, when someone asked about Rastafarianism, the answer sounded very Christian.

While silence may be classless, it isn't always easy. On the table in the centre of our circle, we had a Bible, *Quaker Faith and Practice* and *Advices and Queries*. We also had a few other books which seemed relevant to me. I invited anyone who was finding the silence hard to have a look at these. One was *The Book of Uncommon Prayer,* prayers written by staff and inmates in Grendon and Spring Hill Prisons. It is edited by Jane Bidder, writer in residence. I often read one of her prayers, particularly if the meeting felt restless:

> If you find it hard to pray,
> Just hear what silence has to say.
> Chose your eyes and empty your head —
> You could be surprised at what is said
> Inside your heart and inside your mind.
> For in prayer, there's a peace you will finally find.

I might have substituted 'silence' for 'prayer' in the final sentence.

Another was *Transcendence,* a book of prayers from people of all faiths, which contains such writings as this from Sri Ramakrishna:

'All children are the same to the father. Likewise all devotees call on God alone, though by different names. They call on one Person only. God is one, but God's names are many.'

Carl frequently read *Quaker Faith and Practice,* sometimes a meaningful section, aloud to us. Others would read from *The Bible*, again sometimes sharing a passage.

I was surprised, though I shouldn't have been, by the popularity of the flowers from my garden which were always in the centre of the table. In my introduction to the silence I always said that as Quakers we believe that there is that of God in everyone.

'We have flowers to remind us that God is in all creation,' Hugh would frequently add.

Men liked to take the flowers back to their cells, sometimes almost quarrelling over them, usually sharing them. Once, when a women officer came to take them back to their wings, Spenser offered her a flower with a deep bow, she put it in her hair.

One day I was stopped by the officer at the gate, 'You can't take flowers into a prison.'

'All churches and chapels have flowers,' I said. Security was called and said flowers could go to the chapel, but not to cells. This caused some anger after meeting, and I was delighted that, when I retired, my successor, knowing nothing of this ruling, allowed flowers to go back to cells .

I remember one group of older men from the Vulnerable Prisoner (VP) Wing, who were mainly farmers. They had requested a silent meeting, though of course it had to be at different time from the meeting for the rest of the prison. They told me how much they appreciated the flowers.

'These flowers are alive, they remind me of home,' said Michael, 'and of my dog.'

'That's what we miss most here: the earth, growing things, the weather,' said John.

Weather seemed important to them. From the VP wing they had to come to the chapel from the open air, and often remarked on it. I realised how important weather is to farmers everywhere. Now, cut off from it for most of the day, they relished any opportunity to be out in it, whatever it was. It sometimes seemed even more important than family. Unlike some relatives, the weather didn't reject them.

'I like coming to the chapel on a Monday afternoon,' said Michael. 'When we come to Sunday Services the rest of the prisoners are on exercise, and they spit at us through the wire.'

Something very special could happen in these silent prison meetings.

'I've got ADHD,' said Fred, 'I've never been in silence for as long as half an hour, but I'll give it a go. Don't think I can sit still, but I'll try.'

To my amazement he succeeded.

As soon as the silence ended he started jumping about, 'I can't believe it,' he said, 'it's amazing. It must've been the silence that did it. It silenced me.'

He came for several weeks, and brought his friends. 'You've got to be quiet and sit still,' he would warn them, 'this is the only time I can be still, don't you go spoiling it for me. And for the others.'

Behind the old chapel was a World Faith Room, which felt very like a Quaker meeting house, and where we used to hold our meetings before the roof started leaking. On the far side of the chapel from the wings, the silence there was disturbed only by the screaming of the seagulls. Many remarked on the quality of the silence in that room: the only place in the prison away from noise.

'I haven't been this quiet for years,' said George.

I have precious memories of many gathered meetings there, and missed it when we moved into the new chapel. The World Faith Room was a small partitioned-off section of the former workshop, with sinks for Muslim ablutions. When we first moved there, there was a heatwave blazing, and this tiny room was unbearably hot; men complained of the smell of Muslim feet. After that we moved our meetings into the main chapel, with its cross and altar, which never felt the same as in the old chapel. Other chaplains and officers often walked through, with varying degrees of respect for the silence; but, just as the darkness cannot put out the light, so our silence conquered these interruptions.

These silences in B prison were by no means unique: many other QPCs tell of similar deep meetings in other prisons. In a lifer prison, now also closed, so many found that their meeting for worship 'spoke to their condition', to paraphrase George Fox, that they joined the Society of Friends, and became

Quakers. That prison meeting became a local meeting, recognised by the area meeting, with members, attenders, their own elders and overseers and, on one occasion, a Quaker wedding. When that prison closed, the members were scattered to various prisons, and something precious was lost. It was a loss also to the Quakers who came from outside to share the meetings.

One of these wrote, 'I always felt that everyone at [that] Meeting was there because it mattered to them very deeply, whether inmates or attenders. As a result our meetings had a depth and resonance which is quite rare in my experience. I still miss it.'

Another said he missed it 'not only for the worship, but also for the opportunity to relate to people who had no other agenda than to be friends. They all enjoyed the chats over tea after meeting—as did we!'

I visited that meeting once with a group from a conference of Quakers in Criminal Justice, which was meeting near by. I was impressed by the number of prisoners attending, around 18, and the depth of the silence. Of course, although Quakers, they couldn't attend area meetings, or other Quaker activities apart from those in the prison, but this might be possible when they moved to a category D prison.

What was it in their 'condition' that made the silence so important? Those in prison are daily confronted with the consequences of past mistakes, of what they have done wrong. Some spoke of an inner 'evil', which might threaten their very existence. To meet with a group which celebrated their essential goodness, and valued them for what they were, must have been healing, not the least to self-respect.

I think prison meetings are special partly because most of those there are going through severe problems; several were accompanied by their ACCT (Assessment, Care in Custody and Teamwork) forms, for those who it was felt might be at risk of suicide or self-harm (see *Chapter 6*). The silence was not just a soothing peace, but something positive in lives when all must seem negative. I think I felt something similar in meetings for worship which my area meeting used to organize once a month outside a local USA Air Force base, where planes took off to bomb Iraq and Afghanistan. The evil there, so close to us, seemed to accentuate the sense of good, or God in our midst. I suspect many of those in the prison meetings felt the same.

When I returned to B prison after a lengthy illness, during which a C of E chaplain, at the request of some of the men, had been organizing the meetings, I was touched by the support from those who remembered me. I felt truly 'held in the light', to use another Quaker phrase.

I shall always remember those meetings in B prison. I'm grateful to all who participated, making these half hours a time where we were able, in the words of *Quaker Advices and Queries*, to 'discover a deeper sense of God's presence.' I think we found 'a gathered stillness' where we felt 'the power of God's love drawing us together and leading us.' I think we all felt 'the evil weakening in [us] and the good raised up.'

Over the years, with the constantly changing population of a local prison, very many men must have joined us. I hope the silence gave them something to help them to get through their imprisonment, if not 'to help them lead law-abiding and useful lives in custody and after release'.

CHAPTER FOUR

A Confession

'Respect the laws of the state but let your first loyalty be to God's purposes. If you feel impelled by strong conviction to break the law, search your conscience deeply'.

Quaker Advices and Queries, No. 35

In 1960 I spent ten days as an inmate of W prison. One Saturday I disobeyed an order of the Metropolitan Police Commissioner prohibiting demonstrations in Trafalgar Square. This was at the height of the first wave of the Campaign for Nuclear Disarmament (CND), when thousands were marching from Aldermaston to London every Easter. That Saturday, the police commissioner's order was also disobeyed by thousands; hundreds were arrested. Most were bailed to appear in court the following Monday when they were fined. The Committee of 100, an off-shoot of CND, founded by Bertrand Russell, which urged non-violent civil disobedience as well as demonstrations, suggested that when arrested we should refuse to give our names and addresses 'to see what would happen'. We must have realised that we would be imprisoned, but I think we were foolish enough, or naïve enough, to believe that, if enough of us did this, we would 'fill the gaols' and embarrass the government. I was one of that group; of course, we were remanded in custody, most of us over the weekend and were also fined. I was one of a few who were remanded to appear before a magistrate who was about to go on a week's holiday. So we were remanded for ten days.

This was a shock. I'll never forget the degrading, dehumanising process of reception that so many prisoners describe. Having one's clothes and all one's belongings, taken away, ones hair scrutinised for lice, being locked-up for what seemed hours in a sort of swimming pool cubicle. I decided I could cope no longer; besides I needed to be at the girls secondary modern school, where I'd just started my first teaching job, on Monday morning. So I gave the authorities the particulars they wanted, assuming I would then be freed.

'You've been remanded in custody for ten days, so you stay in custody for ten days,' said the officer.

As the cell door finally banged shut on me, I experienced the terror of the first-time prisoner: total helplessness. Never before had I been confronted with a door I couldn't open. A sociology graduate, who'd studied criminology, I was experiencing the reality, rather than the theory, of crime. Used to making my own decisions, being in control of my life, this experience of total powerlessness was overwhelming. I'd chosen to take part in the Committee of 100's experiment, just as some criminals may choose crime, but I'd assumed I could reverse the decision if I so chose. Choice was now denied me, like all criminals I'd lost the power of choice. That was terrifying.

I was locked up for the first, and last, time in my life. It's hard to describe what this feels like. A physical terror hit me in the stomach, and made me feel weak and worthless. Cut off from all contact with fellow human beings, but hearing sounds all around of pain and indifference, I was alone in a totally new way. I was acutely aware of the spyhole, knowing I could be looked in on at any moment, but was unable to look out. This was a new kind of inequality for me. Many of those I later met in B prison told me that after the first time there is no shock. Prison loses its terror and, with that, any deterrent value it may have. But the first experience of this aloneness, listening to the clanging doors, the cries of the other women, unable to be part of whatever was going on outside, was to me a very new kind of claustrophobia, unique to the prisoner.

Once the first shock had worn off, I started to write down my experiences on the greyish, scratchy prison toilet paper, each sheet stamped 'Government Property'. I had no other paper, and was not there long enough to buy any through the canteen system. 'Writing on toilet paper is a punishable offence,' said an officer. I wasn't deterred, and wrote everyday. I wasn't punished, so that's a prison experience I can't write of. I still have the toilet paper: as I read the flimsy sheets, those ten days come back to me.

The sudden loss of control over one's life is in some ways similar to being in hospital, the difference being that in a hospital the staff are on one's side. Increasingly that may be becoming the case in prisons, but in 1960 that wasn't what it felt like in W prison. A fellow Committee of 100 member wrote a poem about his time in prison, which contained the line:

'Don't take you hat off, officer, your humanity shows.'

In B prison I frequently saw the humanity of officers, but I don't remember much from W. There I had a fleeting and superficial experience of the arbitrary nature of prison life. I read the Prison Rules that I'd been issued with, and when I wanted to complain about something in the vegetarian diet I asked to see the medical officer, as the rules stated.

'You'll need to see the governor about that,' she said.

'But the rules say the medical officer.'

'Those rules are out of date.'

'What in heavens name is the use of giving us out of date rules?' I wrote on my toilet paper. Men I met years later complained frequently of requests being arbitrarily rejected: of personal belongings taken away; applications that took weeks to be considered, and were then refused; removal to a distant prison far from relatives, who might no longer be able to visit; training opportunities closed down at a moment's notice; classes discontinued for financial reasons. Sam wanted his guitar which had been allowed in his last prison, but not in B. Often these arbitrary decisions would affect someone's whole life and liberty.

I managed, I'm not sure how, to get a message through to the head of my school. I was told later that she'd been telling the girls in assembly about our demonstration, comparing us to the suffragettes, of whom she was a great admirer. She returned to her office after assembly to a message that one of her probationary teachers was in prison for a week. She could do no less than give me a week's leave of absence without pay.

This has been my guilty secret throughout my years as a prison teacher and a prison chaplain, revealed only to one of the Buddhist chaplains I got to know. Every time I had to fill in a CRB (Criminal Records Bureau) form I admitted to having a record for disobeying the Metropolitan Police Commissioner's orders, but there was never a question about whether I had been imprisoned. So I never mentioned it; I don't know if it would have affected my chance of employment had I done so. Perhaps after so many years, it's time for me to come clean.

Did this experience have anything to do with my decision to teach in a prison and later to accept the nomination to be my area meeting's QPC?

Probably more important was my history of rebellion at my Quaker boarding school, where I was desperately unhappy. I expressed my unhappiness in bad behaviour, disobedience, swearing, breaking rules. I remember one evening when I was eleven or 12, my form mistress sent me to bed early because, 'You're not fit to mix with the other children in your form.' Neither teachers nor prefects seemed to understand my unhappiness. They could only see naughtiness which had to be punished. In other circumstances I might well have found myself in a young offender institution, or approved school as they were then called. I'm sure it was partly this experience that made me a life-long rebel, defender of the underdog and disaffected, but the prison experience may have been a factor.

In W prison I chose to work, though as a remand prisoner I didn't have to, just to get out of my cell. With a group of other women and teenagers, I spent some hours each day dismantling old telephones. None of us knew if some use was going to be made of the parts we separated, or if this was just an occupation for us, like the Victorian crank. Some of the girls had absconded from borstal, they seemed like the children I should have been teaching. They were also very like the men I would meet later in B prison, but here we really were on equal terms. I listened to them as they discussed being sent back to borstal, and noted in my diary, 'They seem very calm, wondering how much of their lives the state will steal.'

I remember one older woman, who proudly showed me her cell. Somehow she'd got curtains for the windows, a piece of carpet on the floor and an armchair.

'The screws always keep this cell for me when I get out,' she said, 'they know I'll be back. This is my home.' This was a Victorian prison, but not overcrowded, no-one shared a cell, in fact one whole landing was unused, its cells empty. So, while I had to 'slop-out' my chamber pot each morning, I didn't have to use it in front of a stranger.

I lay awake at night listening to the shouted 'G'd nights' echoing from cell to cell, and across the yard. 'G'd night Anita.' 'G'd night Eileen.' 'Sleep well.' 'God bless.' One night an officer commanded them to be quiet. After a few minutes it started again, 'G'd night, love.'

My letters were read. I know, because in one I had made disparaging statements about the chapel service on Sunday. The next Sunday I was not unlocked to go to chapel, although I'd put my name down. I remember looking angrily at the door as the shrill sounds of hymns penetrated the walls.

'You didn't seem to value it last week,' the officer said, when I complained.

'Did I write about the girl in the pew in front of me who was inserting swear words into the hymns?' I wrote on my toilet paper. How could I, years later, be part of the official provision of religion in a prison?

As a Quaker, I claim that there is that of God in all: in our prison meetings I spoke of our testimony to equality, represented by the circle we sat in. Yet I was never again so close to those whom Gandhi called Harijans, 'children of God', as I was in W prison. I am still a rebel, but am fortunate that this has not led me to prison on the other side of the door again. Perhaps deterrence works. From then on I was one of those with keys.

I think I saw briefly some of the same caring that went on in B prison, in the conversations between the young girls all those years ago in W. I wonder if these relationships went beyond the gate. My toilet paper diary records small fights with the authority of the officers. 'My anti-screw attitude is becoming more violent every day,' I wrote, 'and with it my relations with other prisoners is improving. I've promised to think of them, pray for them, write to the papers about them when I get out.' I wonder if I did. I never got close enough in that brief time to want to visit or write to any of them. Had I been a chaplain then, this wouldn't have been allowed.

CHAPTER FIVE

Learning in Prison

'The prisoner is never only a criminal and nothing else...it is good to think more of what the man may become than of what he is.'

Archbishop William Temple, *Ethics of Punishment*, 1930

In the 1980s I spent about five years teaching basic education in D prison. As in B prison, I learned far more than I was able to teach. D was quite different from B prison: I think the education we offered was also very different from prison education today. In the 21st-century education in prisons has become 'learning and skills', with the emphasis very much on skills, particularly those that will help the students to find work when they get out. There seems little left from the cuts beyond basic skills. In D prison we interpreted education broadly: we took students out into the countryside to write poetry; made videos; organized a mock election (won by the Monster Raving Loony Party on a platform of votes for prisoners); invited speakers from outside on a variety of topics, including local charities and speakers on world faiths; showed films such as *Gandhi*; organized an Asian Day involving curries cooked by the students and Asian music; ran a sewing group where students made soft toys for their children or to be sold for charity; put on plays, including a pantomime, for others in the prison; grew organic toma- toes; made a sundial and much else in the name of basic education. Amid all this, students learned to read and write, gained qualifications in communi- cation skills and learned English as a second language. These were the days before SATs or benchmarks.

I was fortunate to be involved in the first venture into full-time basic education in D prison. Before that it seems to have been assumed that as men came to an open prison towards the end of long sentences, they would have done education earlier in their prison career; however, increas- ingly, short-term prisoners were also being sent to D prison. Additionally, it catered for middle-class, white-collar, offenders: estate agents, accountants, and other professionals, many of whom came to evening classes (an early victims of the cuts in B prison). I taught an O level sociology evening class before basic education.

Thomas was an accountant who wanted to become a teacher after his release. 'I think sociology will be useful to me. I've got a place in a college of education for when I get out. I've been totally honest about my background,' he said, 'they were really understanding and supportive. So were the prison, I got a day's release for the interview.' It's obviously easier for the middle-class criminals to get back into society after crime, I thought. Then, just before his release date, the college informed him that they had withdrawn their offer, ostensibly to protect the other students.

Thomas was devastated, 'I'm not a paedophile,' he said. 'I could've made maths really interesting with my knowledge of the financial system.'

Later in B prison I was to hear so many similar stories of employers, girl-friends, landlords who'd said they'd stand by a prisoner, only to change their minds when release was imminent.

The terms in D prison were only ten weeks long; the first group of students understood that they would only have one term, but they were enthusiastic to continue. In the final week they organized a tea party for the governor and senior staff. They baked cakes, brewed tea, and made a speech of thanks for what education we were able to offer in the time available, and asked for more. They even composed a poem, part of which went:

Ten weeks isn't long
To learn all we can
Ten weeks in a classroom
But we've learned to a man

One word
Our times tables
How to fill in those forms
Learning everyday functions
Just like the norms

We may be the deviants
And we know we've been bad
But education's helped us
Get back what we had.

This was carefully written out in calligraphy by a friend of one of the students, read out and then presented to the governor. I couldn't believe my ears listening to his response. In his defence, he was nearing retirement.

'I left school at the age of 14 and it never did me any harm,' he said, 'don't forget you're here to be punished, not educated.'

The next term we had a different group of students.

We found poetry a useful way of teaching literacy, and published booklets of students' writing. This was written by an elderly Sikh, who was studying English as a second language. My 'thought about prison' is very similar to his:

Tomorrow will be my last day in prison.
What a beautiful world outside prison.
The same day when I was pushed in prison
What I lost when I got in the prison.
No one knew what was my thought about prison.

It was my thought all bad people are in prison.
But my mind changed after a few days in prison.
Some people are very beautiful, but they are in prison.
Some people are very bad but they are not in prison.

Sometimes we wrote joint poems as a whole class exercise, which seemed to work remarkably well, it used whatever literacy skills each one had, and involved valuable cooperation. One winter day when the trees were sparkling with hoarfrost, my class were outside waiting for me when I came in, anxious to get into the warm.

'Look at that, Mary, we must video this,' they said, pointing to the trees. We did, and they wrote poems. Later, when the spring came we videoed daffodils and primroses, again they wrote poetry. Eventually we had a video called, 'The Four Seasons', with the students (and me) learning to edit the footage.

Winter

White branches, like Jack Frost's fingers
All ragged and spread
Causing cold pains
As the flakes fall.

Feet like ice, crunching the cold snow
Crackling like cornflakes
As the mist falls

And the birds all fly into the trees
With white fingers,
And they're all huddled together
Like black holes
For Jack Frost to operate.

Spring

Daffodils standing like soldiers in the morning sun,
With their heads bowed down.
The trumpet like flowers
Simulating a fanfare
To welcome the early spring.

The violets nestling like tiny jewels
Between and under the bracken bed of winter.

The water in the lake still cold and uninviting
But it's home for the ducks and fish
Who had been waiting for the spring.

It's surely a good time to be alive.

One of our visiting speakers was a poet, who had parented over a dozen 'hard to foster children', the kind of children who might well have ended-up in prison had they not had her as a foster mother. She wrote poems about her work, and we invited her to read and talk about them with our students. One poem brought tears to some eyes; many had experienced local authority care.

In Care

This child, he says,

Meaning this person whom I love,

This child

Is in Care.

And decisions will be taken

On his behalf

By the appropriate authorities.

In Care?

Whose care?

Who cares

For him?

I love him, I say,

Meaning I care

Whether he is sad or happy

Whether he is well or ill

I care.

Oh no, he says,

You do not understand

This child

Is in Care.

He is in all particulars

The property of the state

Whose appointed representative

Is, in this instance,

My humble self.

In short

I am his keeper.

In Care?
Whose care?
Who cares for him?

You have not lain awake, I say,
At night, and cried for him.
You have not worried
That he might be hungry
Or have chilblains on his toes.
You have not waited through the year
And had the strength to let him be.

This child, he says,
Is in Care.
All decisions will be taken
On his behalf
By the appropriate authorities.

Oh Christ, why can't they let him be?

Our students might well have wished they had had this poet as a foster mother. None of her children, now all adults, with their own children, have become one of the one in three prisoners who started life in care and now find prison almost a natural home.

Working in D prison I quickly found that the Quaker concept of the 'Inner Light' applied to all the men I had the privilege of teaching. When I asked them why they had chosen education when they could have earned more doing a job, almost all replied, 'Because I'm thick, miss.' In nearly every case this wasn't true. I also realised that everyone has the capacity to change. I don't know why this surprised me, it is the basis of education, and all faiths, including Quakerism. Education is about change: learning to be different, not the same person with the ability to read and write, but a new person. This was our aim in the education department at D. I think it's something 'learning and skills' departments ignore, with their emphasis on training, involving much more limited change.

Charlie was one who changed, I met him early on in D prison. An elderly man, coming to the end of a life sentence, he filled a pile of exercise books with his rather pathetic life story. It started with him writing, 'I wasn't there when she was killed'. A couple of books later this became, 'I didn't mean to kill her, but she wouldn't pull her pants down.' Finally he wrote, 'I'm sorry I killed her.' When in a prison for lifers, which he could not praise too highly, Charlie had started painting.

He won prizes at the annual Koestler Exhibition for prisoners' art, which enabled him gradually to be able to say, 'I'm an artist,' rather than, 'I'm a criminal, a murderer.' This was the theme of his autobiography. Many sneered at his rather primitive pictures, but this didn't shake his belief in his changed status. There must be more like Charlie, I thought, and started looking for others; I found many. I talked to them at length, and to others in any prison where I could get an invitation from a member of the education staff and eventually wrote a book on the subject: *Inside Art.*

I wondered if there could be some link between being an artist and being a criminal, and originally subtitled the book 'Creativity and Crime'; this was altered by the publishers to 'Crime, Punishment and Creative Energies.' To investigate this I interviewed 30 artists who had won some award: either a Koestler Award, or one from a local arts organization. I included music and writing as arts. The Koestler Exhibition now has 58 diverse art forms. Ten of my artists were in prison, ten had once been in prison and ten had, so far as I knew it, never been to prison. I asked them about their childhoods and found them similar: anarchic, wild, rebellious, bunking-off school.

They all tended to feel they were different from other children, and that there was something within them that impelled them to be creative. Jim said, 'I know I've got something there and it's worth doing, so I enjoy it, and it gives me that sort of uniqueness to myself which everyone needs … you need that sort of lump inside you.'

None of the two prisoner groups had been to art school, most of those in the non-prison group had. The latter had their gifts recognised earlier, and were more likely to be middle-class.

I asked them about their feelings during and motivations for creativity, and was not surprised to find these differed. For many of those in prison, including Charlie, art was an escape from the prison environment. He said, 'When I'm painting?… I'm at ease… I'm in a different world that nobody really knows about … I'm not in prison … my body's here, but my mind and spirit's where the pictures are, in that world of, you might say Paradise.'

When I asked him what it felt like to be in Paradise, he replied, 'Terrific. Peaceful. It's heavenly bliss, and it feels good. You're in a different world where everything is happy, and everybody's pleased to see you. It's a different world altogether.'

However, the conclusion I reached from my conversations, was that individuals can and do change, not that artists are different: we all have creative energies within us, all are potential artists.

The transforming power of art is similar to the transforming power of faith or of education. All involve connecting to our inner being, what Quaker's call the 'Inner Light'. A chaplain must believe in change, in redemption, the possibility of turning lives around. In theory this is also the aim of the Prison Service, which prioritises 'reducing re-offending'. But all too often it seems that prison staff, sometimes including chaplains, talk as if they didn't really believe this. I was frequently told by another chaplain, 'You must remember, Mary, these men are in prison for a reason.' Back in the 1980s I, and I think most of the education staff in D prison, believed we could help in changing lives. The students seemed to believe in it too.

I've heard that in Learning and Skills departments in 21st-century prisons, art and other creative activities were early victims of cuts. The annual Koestler Exhibition of prisoners' art continues at the Royal Festival Hall each autumn with around 20,000 visitors; in 2013 they received over 7,000 entries, but for the first time this was down on the previous year's figure of over 8,000. Twenty years ago it was around 4,000. However, I suspect most of this work today is now done in individuals' cells, without the support of art classes or teachers. Qualifications that are seen to lead to employment are now the first priority. Yet in my research I talked to ten men who had started their artistic careers in prison, and went on to be successful artists when they got out. Some of them making a good income, as well as not re-offending, and living fulfilling lives.

Being creative is part of being human, whether described as the Quaker

Inner Light, or Churchill's 'treasure ... in the heart of every person'. It is being 'involved in mankind', and involved in the care for, and of, our fellow human beings. We all need this in our lives, in our education system, in our society and in our prisons.

CHAPTER SIX

Death in Prison

'Any man's death diminishes me, because I am involved in mankind, and therefore
never send to know for whom the bells tolls; it tolls for thee.'

John Donne, *Meditation*, xvii

When I agreed, perhaps too willingly, to be the area meeting's QPC, and
to try to take some Quaker ethos into the prison, there were many things I
should have thought about, but didn't. I didn't realise that this might involve
requests for vocal prayer (see *Chapter 2*). Nor did I understand that I would
need to come to terms with death. I'd always thought, carelessly perhaps,
that one day I'd discover if there's an afterlife, but, for now, I felt it more
important to concentrate on this life. I still believe this, but now I understand the Quaker query:

'Are you able to contemplate your death and the death of those closest to you?
Accepting the fact of death, we are freed to live more fully.'

Quaker Advices and Queries No. 30

Our life is enriched by contemplating death and accepting its reality.

One of the duties of chaplains is to break bad news to prisoners; the chapel
is a better place to do this than a shared cell or crowded landing. For some
a visit from a chaplain always means bad news. One year, when distributing
Christmas cards, Kevin greeted me with, 'Thank God that's all. I thought
it must've been bad news.'

The most common bad news we had to pass on was the death of a family
member. As a volunteer I was only asked to do this when I was the sole chaplain in the prison, which happened regularly in my early days.

The first time I had to tell a man that his grandmother had died shocked my complacency. Grandmother, I thought, probably elderly, possibility sick. Not a close relation. But Sam's nan had brought him up, and was closer to him than his parents.

'I'd rather it'd been my Mum,' he said.

I learned later that this is common: nan is often closer than parents, sometimes an escape from parents. Those in prison can only go to the funeral of a close relative: child, parent, sibling. Nans are not included.

I asked a governor if Sam could go to her funeral, 'To him she was his mother.'

'He'll only be allowed to go if there's a formal document stating that his grandmother was *in loco parentis*.'

Of course there was no such document. So Sam couldn't say goodbye to Nan with the rest of the family at her funeral. All we could offer him, and others in his position, was a chance to come into the chapel at the time of the funeral, light a candle and be there 'in spirit'. Some refused this, others came and prayed, and wept, as Sam did.

One of the Friends who came regularly to our silent meetings was called Nan. We always started a meeting with each of us introducing ourselves. More than once when we were going round the circle and Nan said, 'I'm Nan,' someone would say, 'Really? Is that your name? Are you a nan?'

I've never met anyone whose name was Mum, but I thought the name Nan seemed as unlikely to some as being called Mum.

While I don't remember ever having to tell someone their Mum had died, I do remember telling two very different men of the deaths of their fathers.

Wayne was brought to the chapel by a prison officer; he had hardly come through the door before saying, 'Is it one of the children?'

'No, it's your father.' He was so relieved that nothing had happened to his children he seemed not to care about his father's death.

'I haven't seen him for years.'

He didn't want to go to the funeral, and when I asked if he would like to light a candle and pray, he wanted to pray for his children. I'm sure he grieved later.

David reacted totally differently; he seemed to have no idea why I was taking him to the chapel, and when I told him, he refused to believe it.

'We're not allowed to give bad news without first checking with the hospital or undertaker. I spoke to a nurse who was with him when he died. She said to assure you it was very peaceful.'

'Why was he in hospital?'

Stupidly I hadn't asked. I promised to ring again.

Suddenly, realising that his father was indeed dead, David exploded in anger, possibly mixed with guilt: he jumped up and started charging round the chapel kicking the walls, throwing chairs, banging his head against the walls and the floor and screaming.

I think this was the only time in my years in the prison that I nearly felt afraid. Momentarily I considered calling an officer, the wing office was just outside the chapel; I even thought of pressing the large green panic button. It didn't take me long to decide not to: David needed to do this, he didn't need to be restrained by officers, and take his anger back to his cell, or worse still, the segregation block. So I sat quietly and waited. After some minutes he picked up one of the chairs he'd knocked over, sat down and started to sob. Remembering that the chapel is the only place in a prison where it's safe to cry, I was thankful I hadn't sent for help. I found the tissues. I wondered if I should go and sit beside him, not sure if he needed my presence. He wept unrestrainedly for some time, during which I thought I sensed prison officers peering in through the spyhole. Had they heard his anger through the double doors? I willed them to go away, and, if they had been there, they did. Finally David came towards me and said, 'Sorry.'

I wasn't sure if it was the tears or the anger he was apologising for.

'That's all right, that's what the chapel's for.'

He spent some time slowly going round, picking up the chairs and eventually came and sat beside me.

'Tell me about your father.'.

He talked for a long time. He told me of fishing trips to the local canal, learning to swim, and to steal. He started slowly, then more animatedly, smiling, later even laughing. After a time I asked him, 'Would like to light a candle for your father, perhaps say a prayer?'

'Yes ... Does it matter if I don't believe?'

'No. Of course not. I'm a Quaker: we don't have any set form of words I could offer you, but we can give thanks for your father's life. Can we have some silence to do this in? Then you might like to say something for your dad. Or I can if you'd like that.'

I think we both said some words before he blew out the candle and said, 'I'll go back to my cell now, please.' As we parted, he shook my hand and thanked me. I'm not sure what for. I promised I'd leave a message for the chaplain on duty the next day to help him make his application to go to the funeral, and warned the officers on his wing that he could be in a volatile state. They promised to keep in eye on him.

It occurred to me later that David seemed to have gone through what are known as the four 'stages of grief' in less than an hour: disbelief, anger, grief, acceptance. He probably went through them many more times, as I believe most people do. When I went to see him the next week, he'd gone to another prison, so I never knew if his application to attend the funeral was granted. It may have been too far away; even the funeral of a close relative is not guaranteed, it depends again on staff availability and the costs involved.

Death is never far from the prison wall. Many men came to the chapel to light a candle, say a prayer or just sit quietly on the anniversary of the deaths of loved ones: parents, children, partners, siblings, friends.

'This is the anniversary of the day my Dad topped himself in this very prison,' said a man I didn't know whom I met by chance on a landing.

'Would you like to come to the chapel and think about him, say a prayer or light a candle?'

'No. I don't think so.' The chapel doesn't appeal to all in prison.

'Today is the anniversary of the death of my baby,' said John, in tears, in the silence of our meeting. Afterwards more than one of the group said their children, or children close to them, had died cot deaths.

I could only guess at the pain of living through such anniversaries away from the support of family and loved ones.

As a sociology student, nearly 60 years ago, I'd learned that working-class people live shorter lives than those of the middle-classes. In B prison I got to know those who died the youngest.

'I was in a gang of six when I was at school,' said Spenser, 'I'm the only one still alive.'

I was horrified. 'What happened to the others?'

'Drugs. Stolen cars. Alcohol. Violence.'

The suicide nets must have been daily reminders of the prison's duty not to let men die. I met many men 'on an ACCT', what is commonly known outside as 'suicide watch'. It stands for: Assessment, Care in Custody and Teamwork. Those thought to be at risk of self-harm or suicide are closely monitored, and observations logged in a book, which follows the prisoner wherever he goes. Anyone who has any contact with him has to write their comments in this book, which is passed from officer to teacher, to doctor, to chaplain, and back to the officer. You weren't supposed to write anything you wouldn't be happy for the man himself to read. I made many entries in such books, and did some basic ACCT training. I thought I was supposed to discuss with the man what I was going to write. Most of my entries read, 'Came to the silent meeting.' I would ask him if he'd like me to say anything more, and sometimes added such comments as: 'Found it helpful,' or 'Participated in the discussion,' or even 'Spoke during the silence.' Sometimes, 'Found it hard.'

The book was an opportunity for interaction between prisoners and staff. Men had to be asked if they wanted to go on an ACCT, and were consulted when it might no longer be necessary. When the ACCT replaced the former '20.52' system of surveillance of suicide risks, which seemed more about surveillance than interaction, numbers of prison suicides fell, only to rise again, as overcrowding in prisons meant that more and more were spending time in police cells on being sentenced rather than in prison. The first few days inside are a time of greatest risk; a prison can do more to help the prisoner then than a police station. Shortly before B prison closed, the VP unit was turned into a special first night wing, where new prisoners could be introduced gradually to prison life and treated with care. The VPs dispersed to other prisons, which made visiting harder for some relatives.

When a close relation died, men were allowed to make a phone call from the chaplaincy office, and sometimes have an extra, 'compassionate' visit. Philip was distraught when I went in answer to his request to see a chaplain.

'My girlfriend's lost our twins.' After a moment I realised he was talking about a miscarriage, not losing them in a supermarket.

'How far on was her pregnancy?'

'Twenty weeks.'

To Philip these precious foetuses were already his children. 'I need to talk to my girlfriend,' he begged. I decided he'd been bereaved and took him to the office and dialled the number he gave me, trying not to listen to his tearful half of the conversation. When he finally put the phone down, he said, 'She's really upset.'

'I'm not surprised.'

'She needs to see me.'

'When's your next visit?'

'I saw her only last Saturday. I can't wait till Saturday week. She can't. I really need to see her. She'll do something desperate if I don't. I know she will. I know her. She needs me.'

'Perhaps we can arrange a compassionate visit,' I said. I soon found the limits of compassion in the eyes of the prison authorities.

'It wasn't children, only a miscarriage.'

'To him, and to his girlfriend, they were babies.' The visit never happened, and I lost touch with Philip.

For some of course, death was the cause of their being in prison. Those who kill are always sent first to the nearest local prison, to await trial. After sentence they go to a training prison, are given a sentence plan and begin to serve the long years to which society condemns them for the taking of life. We had few lifers in B, apart from those recalled from D for some misdemeanour.

'The army taught me how to kill. It didn't teach me what else to do with my anger,' said William, awaiting trial for murder. I met many ex-servicemen, who spoke highly of the work of the British Legion in supporting them and their families while they were in prison. But the number of such men made me wonder if the armed services do enough to prepare redundant servicemen for civilian life. The change must be like coming out of prison, with similar problems. One in three of those in prison spent time in local authority care as children, and for some the time between care and prison was spent in the services. They had never faced the problems of living outside an institution, or forming relationships. As Jason (see *Chapter 7*) said, 'I grew up in a kids home. I never learned to make friends.'

In my years in B prison, there were several deaths in custody: some suicides, some natural causes. Both meant the whole prison was distressed, particularly on the wing where the man had died. I never had to talk to an officer who had found a man hanging, but the Free Church chaplain told me of her experience of this. The officer was distraught, not sure if he needed to take time off to be away from the prison, or to get back to work as quickly as possible. The chaplain said she didn't know what to suggest, but knew she had to let him talk for as long as he needed. So she listened as he told her how he'd cut the man down with his fish knife, and of the futile attempts to resuscitate him. Then she rang me and I knew I had to listen. I then rang one of my support group, who was a supervisor for Cruise counsellors, and who did the same for me. Other chaplains seemed to lack a system for supervision. One told me his fellow clergy would listen if he needed this, but mostly he relied on prayer. My area meeting wisely now make a 'support person' for QPCs an official appointment of the meeting.

Eric taught me a great deal about death. He was a gentle man; though he would say he wasn't religious in any way, he was deeply spiritual. He came regularly to the monthly silent meeting for VPs. Several of this particular group, including Eric, were scientists or deeply interested in science. After the silence, we frequently discussed the relationship between science and religion, how both are based on doubt and uncertainty, not at loggerheads, as some popular scientists seem to believe. Eric was the only person I've met who had not only read Stephen Hawking's *Brief History of Time* but understood it. He tried, but failed, to explain it to me, the book is still beyond me.

For a few months Eric was missing from our meetings, and I assumed he'd got out. Then his friend Bill told me that he'd developed secondary cancer and was too weak to reach the chapel.

'I was once a hospital porter,' he said, 'I'm sure Eric's had a recurrence of the cancer he had a few years ago, it's already returned once. I've told the officers, but they wouldn't listen. I even went to healthcare, but as far as they're concerned I'm just a con.'

I visited Eric in his cell for some weeks, and remember having a silent meeting in the nearby adjudications room. Then I saw him in the healthcare centre of the prison. Finally I heard he'd been transferred to the oncology ward of the local hospital. When first I saw him there, he seemed much better. He was still very weak and attached to various drips, with oxygen to help him breathe, yet he was being guarded by two prison officers. When I remarked on this he said, 'My daughters persuaded them to take the handcuffs off.'

We talked about what might happen after death. I quoted the song by Ewan McColl, written when he realised he'd not much longer to live,

The Joy of living
Scatter my dust and ashes, feed me to the wind
So that I may be
Part of all you see
The air you are breathing,
I'll be part of the curlew's cry and the soaring hawk,
The blue milkwort and the sundew hung with diamonds.
I'll be riding the gentle wind that blows through you hair,
Reminding you how we shared
In the joy of living.

'I think I'll be going back to where I was before the Big Bang,' said Eric.

Next week I was shocked to find him near death in a side ward. He'd decided there was no point in delaying his end, and asked for treatment to be stopped. He was very weak, hardly able to speak. I heard little of what he said, but managed to make out: 'Funny old world ... funny way to go.' Then he was obviously trying to say something important, and after I had asked him to repeat it twice, one of the prison officers said, 'He said, "Don't look so solemn, Mary".'

I smiled at him, and he smiled back. He died later that day.

The next meeting for the VPs was a moving occasion, although not many of those attending remembered Eric. Bill brought in an extra chair—for Eric—who was a real presence at the meeting.

I had a letter from the governor saying Eric's family wanted to thank me for the comfort and compassion I showed him when he was dying. I wanted to write back, and tell them about the Eric I had known, who had come to silent meetings and discussed science.

'The family want closure, and nothing more to do with the prison,' said the family liaison officer. So I was not allowed to know their address. It's not only prisoners who find prison a frustrating place.

Eric taught me so much about death: we don't need to look 'solemn' in the face of it. It's as natural as birth, and as universal. As John Donne said, 'Anyone's death diminishes me, because I am involved in mankind'. We need to accept death, contemplate it, that we may 'live more fully'.

CHAPTER SEVEN

Christmas in Prison

Will You Be Home For Christmas, Dad?
I'd never cared for Christmases
I'd found them dull and boring;
All those aged in-laws
With their knitting and their snoring.

There were lights and lots of glitter,
And the presents weren't so bad,
But all our fuss and bickering
Would drive our parents mad.

It grew worse when I married
So I chose to work away
Content to think my duty done
By phoning Christmas Day.

When my daughter graced the scene
I had to work much more
To pay for cots and clothes and things...
That little ones adore.

It never once did dawn on me
Of all the things she'd had
The Christmas treat she'd wanted most
Was me — her dear old Dad.

I'd come in tired, or drunk, or both
Returning late at night
Forgetting all those little things

Like hugs and tucks-in-tight.

Unaware of all her sorrows
Too blind to see her need
I'd filled my life with rubbish
By giving way to greed.

Her eyes foretold her question
When she came the other day
'Will you be home for Christmas, Dad?
Will you come home to stay?'

I saw how much she loved me
Despite the pain I'd brought
And there contained within her eyes
The answer that I'd sought

I saw the hope of all the world
Within those eyes so brave
And I, a worthless sinner that,
A child came to save.

'Peter' (in D prison, quoted in *Inside Art*)

'Christmas is a dreadful time here,' said James, in D prison. 'We're away from our families, but it's a family festival. We could walk out at any time, and join them.'

'Plenty do,' said Arthur, 'especially just before Christmas, but they always end up back in a cat B prison. That's why we don't, but there's nothing to stop us. No wall.'

'The wall's inside us,' said James, 'it's harder than the wall outside of us. That's why we don't walk out. That's the wall that keeps us in here. I think we feel it most at Christmas.'

D prison's education department had a long Christmas break, when we wouldn't see our students, and the staff were wondering if and how we should celebrate Christmas. One of the teachers had a brainwave, 'Let's celebrate the "Lord of Misrule",' she suggested. She told us that in medieval England a Lord of Misrule was appointed to oversee Christmas festivities. 'I think this often involved making the masters servants while the servants were masters for a day. We could be students for a day, and the students could teach us.'

'Everyone's got something to teach,' she assured the assembled students from all three classes. Most responded positively. The first suggestion was that we teachers should all have to go to the gym for an hour, while the students instructed us. Each day started with an hour's gym for our students. Many objected to this, but it was provided free by prison staff, and meant that students could start the day at the same time as prisoners with jobs, while we teachers could come an hour later.

The idea was taken up enthusiastically by most students, less so by the teachers. We compromised on half an hour of gym, followed by half an hour of yoga for us to recover. I can't remember much of what I learned that day, but I remember an elderly man who said,

'I've spent half my life in prison. What could I teach anyone?'

'What did you do before you were in prison?'

'Gardening.'

'Surely there's something about gardening you could teach us?'

A pause.

'I could show you how to prune roses.'

I've forgotten his name, but I've thought of him every year when I prune my roses, for the last 30 years.

B prison tried to make Christmas as painless as possible. There were Christmas trees on each wing and in the chapel, a good Christmas dinner and more time on association, with table-tennis and snooker tournaments. But in order to give staff more time with their families, visits were curtailed over the holiday period. In the chapel we had a carol service to which we invited the volunteers who came to the various chapel activities, members of the Independent Monitoring Board, Cruise counsellors and others. Some of the Salvation Army band came to play for the carols, their cheerful sounds disappearing into the height of the old chapel, but echoing deafeningly in the smaller new one. The kitchen provided mince pies, and men who came often went out with bulging pockets.

On Christmas morning there was always Catholic mass followed by the Ecumenical Service; once the bishop came to preach at the latter. For a few years the Free Church chaplain and I went to both these services. The Catholics used to bring in a big tin of toffees, which was then left for those coming to the Ecumenical Service. The officers usually brought the men in late, as frequently happened on Sunday mornings, but on Christmas morning it was because they'd enjoyed a cooked breakfast.

Chaplains used to deliver a Christmas card and a diary to each man in the prison. For the first few years I was there these were provided by a Christian charity. The cards were a sheet of A4 folded in half, with a religious Christmas scene on the front, and the two half sides of A4 inside filled with a long letter, which appeared to be handwritten. I assumed they were actually printed, but I was assured that somewhere there were sincere Christians who laboriously wrote out messages to those in prison. I pictured them, filled with goodwill, but not realising that the average reading age of those in prison is around seven. I read a few and saw that the letters varied, they could have been handwritten. All bore a similar message: Christmas celebrates the birth of our Lord, who came to save sinners. The messages mostly went on to tell more of the crucifixion than the nativity of Jesus, with a brief reference to the resurrection, and much exhortation to them to ask Christ's forgiveness, accept Him as Lord, and enjoy a transformed life.

Chaplains are not allowed to proselytise, and I felt this was definitely proselytising. I brought it up at a chaplaincy meeting, where my concern was not well received.

'Christmas is a Christian festival. Surely we can deliver a Christian message at Christmas?'

'But we give them to men of other faiths, and none.'

'They can always refuse.'

I'd had a couple of refusals of the cards, but the diaries were popular, and gratefully received.

'Thanks so much. I've been waiting for that diary,' said Sam.

That year I felt unable to join in the annual distribution, and missed the chance to have a Christmas chat to some of the men I didn't know. I usually said something like, 'I hope you have as good a Christmas as possible.' I was surprised and disturbed by some of the replies.

'I'll have a better time than when I'm on the out. I'll be warm, have a good meal and somewhere to sleep.'

The next year I took my concern about the cards to the governor responsible for the chaplaincy, showing her some of them. She agreed that it was proselytising, and brought it up at the next chaplains' meeting. In future we'd continue to give out the diaries, the pictures of the 'Holy Land' were not seen as proselytising, but a chaplain, who was an artist, would design a card suitable for all faiths. These had something like a star on the front, and the message inside said, 'Season's Greetings from the Chaplaincy Team.'

Discussing the problems of Christmas in prison after a silent meeting produced a range of responses.

'It's dreadful. We miss our children at Christmas, more than any other time.'

'The food's better, and we get more association.'

'We try not to remember it's Christmas, but you can't really.'

'It's a lot of nonsense.'

'It's just another day to be got through. Like any other day.'

After Christmas comes New Year, the time for throwing away calendars. A Friend once asked me if I could use old calendars in the prison. 'I've got one with some really beautiful pictures, it seems a pity to throw it out. Do you think someone might like the pictures in their cell?'

'I'll ask,' I said, 'I'll have to ask security as well as the men.'

Security said, 'As long as there are no names or addresses on them, and you'll have to remove any pieces of wire.' At the next silent meeting the men were enthusiastic. All the lovely pictures went.

'We don't all want nude women on the walls,' said Sam.

After that for several years local Quakers used to give me old calendars. I received large piles of them. It took some time to check for names, and it was often surprisingly hard to take off the wire spirals, sometimes I had to tear each page out separately, but it seemed worth it. When we were moving from the old chapel to the new, I had a large pile of these calendars, waiting my attention. I tried to carry them all to the new chapel, and of course failed. I dropped first one, and then the rest as I tried to pick it up. Immediately I was surrounded by men offering to help. It must have been a time when they were out of their cells to collect a meal, or going to education.

'What are they for?' asked someone.

'They're for people who'd like something other than a nude on their wall.'
'Can I have one?'
'Of course.'
'I don't want nudes,' said another.

In no time I was left with quite a small pile, and didn't need any help to carry them over to the new chapel.

Is this poem, again by Peter, what the prison chaplain hopes for at Christmas?

Give Me Time to Love Him

I'm not confined by handicap, nor crippled by ill-health,
I'm not enslaved by heroin or alcohol or wealth
I am not trapped by poverty or hunger or despair
So I'll speak to you of freedom, of which I have my share.

When they took away illusion and locked me in a cell
I feared I'd lost all dignity, all self-respect as well.
I had to fight self-pity in the squalor and the dust
Not knowing who to turn to, in whom to place my trust.

My life was so much rubbish, pretences had to cease.
Within that empty stillness I found an inner peace
Amongst life's fallen debris the truth was plain to see
For God creates no rubbish — and God created me.

The labourers in the vineyard were paid an equal rate
No matter then my path to God was started somewhat late,
For from that rich and bounteous love, we struggle to deserve,
He gives us time to love him, in trust that time will serve.

Without the office parties and the weight of paper chains
We approach the real Christmas with the freedom that remains
Knowing that the son of God, within the lowly stall
Came to save us sinners, and free us, one and all.

'Peter' (quoted in *Inside Art*)

CHAPTER EIGHT

Stories from Prison

'Are you honest and truthful in all you say and do? Do you maintain strict integrity in business transaction and in your dealings with individuals and organizations?'

Quaker Advices and Queries, No. 37

Quakers have a testimony to truth. Throughout my adult life I have tried to be able to say 'Yes' to the above query, and tend to assume that those I meet are doing the same. In prison I frequently met those who had less respect for the 'truth', or belief in its importance, both staff and prisoners. I was let down time and again by both, particularly prisoners.

Other chaplains frequently told me, 'They're prisoners. They're not in here for nothing. You can't trust what they say.'

But I still tried to believe them when they told me they weren't coming back.

Pete said, 'When I get out this time, I'm going to stay out. This is my last sentence. I'm not coming back. I mean it.'

'What happened, Pete?' I asked, when he reappeared a week or two later.

'Oh well, you know ... life and that ... Whatever,' he said. I think I was sometimes more upset than they were when men returned.

Officers tended to be more cynical about determination not to come back, sometimes also chaplains. My instinct was always, believe prisoners until they proved me wrong, as they so often did.

When officers told me that the men on their wing had changed their minds and no longer wanted to come to the silent meeting, but the next week one of these men said, 'No one came to fetch me last week,' who should I believe? My instinct again said believe the prisoner, which didn't make me popular with staff.

Perhaps the Quaker view of truth is not for general consumption. There are degrees of honesty or dishonesty; a 'white lie' can be more caring, perhaps a different kind of truth. I plead guilty to this. When I started inviting Quakers to come into the meetings each one had to be cleared by the Criminal Records Bureau. This became expensive for the prison, so they decided that visitors who only came occasionally, rather than regularly, didn't need to be vetted, as long as they were never left alone with prisoners. I must never take my eyes off them.

'Do they come in regularly?' asked the security officer, about the list I had submitted of Quakers who would be coming to our meetings.

'No, irregularly.' That is they never came the same week each month, but most came approximately once a month. How do you define 'regular'? Other QPCs told me that in other prisons this meant no more than three times, then they needed security vetting. B's security seemed to accept my definition. Each week I had to give a list of visitors to both the gate and security. They must have seen how often and how regularly each Quaker came, and never questioned it.

'Do they help you in the running of the service?' he asked next.

I thought. They are essential. I couldn't run the meetings on my own. But do they help me, or the meeting? Deciding that we all helped the Holy Spirit, I replied, 'No, they don't help me.'

'They don't read lessons or hand round bread and wine?'

That was easy: Quakers don't have lessons or sacraments, I was on safe ground saying no here.

Nevertheless, I still wanted to believe what I heard from individual prisoners, and what they shared in our discussions after the silence.

As I have mentioned before, one in three of those in prison spent some time in local authority care as children. Children aren't placed in care without good reason; most of those ending up there had suffered in their families. I heard many unhappy accounts of childhood neglect and abuse. It's easier to blame care than one's parents; I heard many sad stories of both. I saw my job as to listen, not to challenge what men chose to tell me; to help them in their 'search for meaning' and to explore 'the human condition' with them. Whatever they told me, I tried always to emphasise the good within them, assuring them that I firmly believe that the light will always triumph eventually over darkness. I tried to 'answer that of God' in them. Here are some of the stories I heard. All were true to those who told them.

Some may object that I am abusing these men's stories, passing on what was told to me as a chaplain. I admit that I am using them but hope this does not amount to abuse. I also hope the stories may highlight some of the problems encountered by those in prison. Do we fully understand that, when we sentence someone to a term of imprisonment, this involves so many more privations and humiliations than the loss of their liberty? These can be loss of jobs, families, homes and lead to depression that drives prisoners to suicide. Are we aware that we frequently lock up the most vulnerable in our society? None of the men whose stories I tell are specific individuals: most are composite portraits, amalgamations of more than one man, or partial stories which I hope will mask identity. Some may seem unique, but their frustrations are typical of those suffered by men I met over the years.

Carl

When I first met Carl he was in a desperate state. He'd tried to kill himself, by cutting his wrists, he was bandaged up, and on an ACCT (see *Chapter 6*). He was in the cell nearest the wing office so that officers could look through his spyhole frequently and make sure he was all right. Carl told me he was in despair because, after years of being in and out of prison, he'd found a wonderful girl, a civil servant, quite unlike the people Carl usually met. She'd said she'd stay with him for as long as he stayed out of trouble, but didn't want to be involved with a criminal. He showed me her picture; I was never sure how they'd met. Carl was determined to go straight for the rest of his life.

'She's a wonderful girl, Sharon, she's never touched drugs.' Drugs were Carl's downfall. 'I started on drugs when I was in my teens, and both my parents died, one after the other the same year. Sharon's like a parent to me. Then I was arrested for something I didn't do. I don't do burglary, Mary. Shoplifting, yes, but not breaking into someone's house. How would you feel if I burgled you?'

There was fingerprint evidence that he'd been in the house that had been burgled, which he didn't deny; he knew the victim of the burglary. But he lived near, and was listed as a 'prolific offender', so was arrested and remanded in custody for about two months. However, Sharon believed his story and stood by him. She knew he didn't do burglary. She told his employer that he was in hospital and his job was held open for him (He had an impressive scar to prove this, which he showed me more than once, it was about a year old, the result of being knifed in a fight). He was eventually, for the first time in his life, found not guilty. However, his employers found out where he had been, and despite doing a lot of driving for them, he had no driving licence, so he lost his job. Once again he turned to drugs and to theft to pay for them. Sharon said that was the end.

'I was in despair, Mary. I went to the river to throw myself in, but then I thought better of it and went to the police station instead and turned myself in. It's not far from the river, the police station.'

A life saved by the position of the police station?

Some time after this he almost succeeded in killing himself. He was unlocked, with all the others on his wing, to collect his lunch, but he didn't join the queue. Instead he hanged himself behind the wing office. An officer, returning for some reason, saw him and cut him down in time with his fish knife. Gradually Carl recovered from Sharon's desertion and started to come to the silent meetings.

'What does it meant to be a Catholic?' he asked me one day, 'I used to go to Catholic church with my Nan when I was a kid. Does this mean I'm a Catholic?'

I wasn't sure, so asked a Catholic chaplain to go and see him. The result was that he decided to become a Catholic, I think largely in memory of his nan. The prison Catholics went to a great deal of trouble to find out that his nan had had him baptised, and he was confirmed in the prison chapel.

Throughout all this he continued to come regularly to our meetings. He used to help me to explain the silence to newcomers, and frequently said, 'I feel more of a Quaker than a Catholic. I don't like being told what I believe.'

Perhaps some Quaker honesty rubbed off on him: the last time he got out he didn't tell me this was his last sentence.

'I'll be back, Mary.' And he was.

'Prison's my only real home now. Know what I mean?' I think I did. I'll never know what became of him when his 'home' closed.

Spenser

'Two men looked out through prison bars
One saw the mud, the other saw stars.'

Based on the words of The Reverend Frank Langbridge (1849-1922) and as used
e.g. by Dale Carnegie in *How to Stop Worrying and Start Living* (5 edn. 2004)

A school friend used to quote this to me around 60 years ago, implying, I
think, that I was the one who saw mud, while she could see the stars. I hadn't
been long in B prison before I told her that from the bars of this prison the
men could see neither mud nor stars. If a prisoner was really determined he
might stand on the bunk, peer upwards through the dirt, and perhaps on a
clear night see what few stars penetrated the light pollution of the city, but
mud: no, only concrete and asphalt. To some, particularly those from rural
environments, the lack of contact with the earth was a real pain added to
their sentence.

One day I went into a cell to find Spenser perched on his bunk, cleaning
the window; probably the first time it had been cleaned in 200 years. He
came down when I came in and said, 'Can you get me some earth?'

'Earth? What do you want earth for?' I was sure this wasn't something a
chaplain was authorised to supply.

'An officer gave me these cuttings. I've had them in water, but look—they're
sprouting roots now. They need soil.'

'Can't you get some yourself when you're out on exercise?'

'Just look at the exercise yard, Mary. It's all asphalt.'

I looked, and saw this was true. Not a weed could grow in that unforgiving
grey. If an officer had given him cuttings, perhaps a chaplain could supply
soil? Next time I came to the prison I brought a small bag of earth from my
garden. Probably wrongly, I didn't check with the gate on the way in, but
thought I ought to ask an officer on the wing. Perhaps it was the same one
who'd provided the cuttings.

'Soil? Why? Who's it for?'

'Spenser.'

'Oh Spenser, yes, that'll be all right.'

Later Spenser showed me the plants which seemed to be thriving, despite their gloomy surroundings.

Spenser was a Muslim. He told me his father was a Muslim and his mother a Catholic — it might have been the other way around. He attended all the chapel could offer: Catholic mass, the interdenominational Sunday Service, the silent meetings and Bible study. Some of the chaplains felt he was just coming to get out of his cell, but his contributions to Quaker discussions suggested he was a genuine seeker. He was a faithful Muslim and took his teabag and biscuits to his cell to eat after sunset during Ramadan.

Winston

Winston was black, and had great charm, which he used to get what he wanted from the system. Sometimes he would have a doctor's appointment or a meeting with his solicitor which clashed with the silent meeting. Somehow, he always managed to persuade the officer returning him to his cell to take him to the chapel instead so he could have some of the meeting, if only the discussion and refreshments. He was in prison several times, always on remand. When he finally came to court he was always found not guilty. 'This has happened so many times, I'm sure its racism. We all know the police are racist. The local cops want me inside,' he said.

'Why don't you move to another area?' I suggested, thinking he could well be right about the racism.

'This is where my families are,' he said, 'why should I let the police drive me out?' I couldn't answer that. He had more than one family, more than one set of children with different mothers.

For a while I didn't see Spenser. Then one day I saw his name again on the list of those who wanted to come to meeting.

'This time it's for something I did do. All that wrongful imprisonment, my solicitor finally got me compensation. Enough to live on comfortably for a bit, and buy a car… I was drinking, innit,' he said, 'it never occurred to me the alcohol'd still be in my breath next morning.'

He seemed as cheerful as he had always been about his wrongful imprisonments.

Christopher

The care which those in prison take of one another, as far as they can, is one of my lasting memories of B prison, and I grew to respect and admire them for this. I first met Christopher when I was 'loitering with intent' when the men were on association.

'Could you come and see Christopher, Miss, I think he could do with seeing a chaplain,' said a man I'd never met before.

I was led to Christopher's cell, which was open like the others, but Christopher wasn't taking advantage of the freedom to mix. He was cowering in a corner, trembling. I was introduced to him by his friend, who then left us together. As he left, Christopher's trembling intensified. When he spoke, and he spoke little at first, his voice was high pitched, like a terrified child.

I gathered later than he'd originally been on the VP wing, as officers thought he might be bullied or even attacked for his childlike behaviour. But he didn't like being with the 'nonces', and asked to be moved to the main prison. Here, far from being attacked, he was protected by his fellow inmates, who did what they could to help him.

I was not the first or the only chaplain to befriend Christopher. He was in the prison for two years or more, and as time went on he told me his story bit by bit. Over time, his trembling grew less, and his voice became more adult. He told me of sexual abuse by an older brother over a number of years.

'I told my Mum, Mary, but she wouldn't believe me, told me not to be silly. One day something snapped, and I set fire to the flat, Mum was nearly killed.'

Arson is a serious offence; the maximum sentence is life. Christopher was in prison many months awaiting trial. One day he was all smiles.

'Good news, Mary. The judge ordered me to be sent to a secure psychiatric hospital until I'm safe to be released.'

'Good news?'

'Yes, yes. It means he thinks I can be cured.'

It was many more months before a secure psychiatric hospital could be found that would take the risk of treating an arsonist, but eventually Christopher left us, and wrote a few letters to the chaplains, saying that he was happy where he had been sent, and being helped.

Christopher said there were demons in his head, who made silence impossible for him, so he couldn't come to the silent meetings, although he managed to do so a few times to please me. 'The demons in my head, Mary, they take me over in the silence.' I tried to persuade him that there was also that of God within him, but the demons were more powerful. I stopped encouraging him to come.

'I love the Sunday Services, Mary. The music can silence my demons.' Evangelical singing has a power which silence doesn't.

'I'll make you a poster for your meetings, if you like,' he offered, 'I'll do it in education, in computer lessons.'

'That'd be lovely, Christopher.'

They were colourful posters and looked good on the wing notice boards, although I'm not sure that they were read any more than my black and white ones. However, the head of Learning and Skills was angry with me for letting him do it. 'He should be doing his course work, not jobs for the chaplaincy,' she said.

I don't think either Christopher or I saw it as a job. I thought back with nostalgia to D prison's education department (*Chapter 5*).

Sean

'Trouble is, I behave like a child,' said Sean, 'like a seven year old.'

Sean and I were discussing the problems he was having trying to establish a relationship with his seven year old son, who, at that time, he was not allowed to see. He showed me the children's books he'd borrowed from the library, to try and get inside the mind of a child of that age. He was re-telling the stories in letters to his son. He'd scant memory of himself at the age of seven.

'I need to grow up,' said Sean. 'It was in an offending behaviour course in another prison I realised I was behaving like a child'.

'We're all behaving like seven year olds,' I told the rest of them. They agreed. I said 'We're afraid to grow up, because we saw grown ups as abusive, frightening, and we didn't want to be like them.' Again everyone agreed. Something frightening/terrible/traumatic had happened to us all between the ages of five and seven: perhaps seeing dad come home drunk, taking the housekeeping money, beating up mum. We'd all decided that we didn't want to be like our fathers.'

Sean linked his problems very clearly to his inadequate, emotionless child-hood, where feelings had little place, 'I've never been hugged in all my life, only abused.' Now, in middle-age, he felt the need both to come to terms with, and find some way to compensate for, this emotional emptiness, to explore his buried, battered emotions.

In the 1960s, his single mother's family rejected her and him because he's half black. He'd spent the years from three to 16 in care, and the rest of his life in and out of prison

'Because I've never managed to grow up,' he said, 'I want, I need to grow up if I'm to have any chance of staying out of prison, but I need help. I want my son to grow up accepting me, and have a relationship with me, which I never had with my dad. I want him to grow up in ways I couldn't. I don't want him in prison.'

Sean was adamant that the crucial age was between five and seven. I wondered if he'd ever read any psychology.

'I don't read much, I'm dyslexic.'

His understanding came from bitter, personal experience, his and that of his peers. He wanted a group where he could have the sort of discussion he'd had in the offending behaviour course.

'I need to be able to talk about my inner feelings, with other men in a similar situation, if I'm ever to grow up ... in that offending behaviour class we discovered that, while our problems were unique to ourselves, we were all very similar. I have a craving for love, like a drug addict's craving. I'm addicted to love; one reason my marriage broke up was because my ex couldn't supply my need. I don't do drugs, but I'm trapped, like an addict. Sometimes, when addicts meet, including me, they feed off each other rather than supporting each other, or they support each other in ways that don't help. You can't talk about this in a group in prison, you can't go back to your cell after a discussion like that, without someone to share the pain. There must be a safety net ... What we need when we get out is an organization for ex-prisoners, like Alcoholics Anonymous, but we're not supposed to meet up with people we knew in prison.'

Sean moved on to another prison shortly after this remarkable conversation. He never came to the silent meetings, though I suggested the discussions could be a place to share his ideas, but he rejected chapel and anything to do with religion, something else that had let him down.

'I'd have to go back to my cell without the safety net,' he said. I hope he found a group to help him grow up.

Jason

'What we need when we get out is an organization for ex-prisoners where we'd support each other,' said Jason. This sounded very like Sean's group, and judging by the success of AA I suspected if such a group could be set up, which several were in later years, it would be equally successful. I'd seen so much mutual support between prisoners.

'The last time I got out the terms of my licence said I mustn't meet the people I'd known in prison. But they're the only ones who'd know what I was feeling.'

The authorities obviously assume that the only interest of those who have been in prison is crime, and more crime. Don't they know how much time those inside spend discussing, worrying and thinking about how they can stay out next time they are released? This came up frequently in our discussions.

'I grew up in a kids home, so I've no friends. I only know those who were in the kids home with me, not friends. I never learned to make friends,' said Jason, now, like Sean, in middle-age. Much of his life since leaving care had been spent in prison. I got to know him through the Pagan chaplain. He came to the silent meeting a couple of times, but it clashed with her visits . She only came every other week, so he would come to our meetings alternate weeks. He told us about Paganism, and was interested in Quakerism. Like so many, it was Quaker openness, lack of a creed, that attracted him. The concept of an Inner Light resonated with his Pagan beliefs.

Ashley

When I first saw Ashley he'd just had a 'Dear John' letter from his girlfriend. 'She's been withdrawing from me since her mother died a while back. But I'm really down. I didn't think it could come to this. I was going to top myself, but my cell-mate found me before I got very far.'

Ashley had been writing poetry, which he hoped he could use when he got out, to help others. 'I'd like to deter kids from crime. This is no way to live,' he said, showing me some of his poems.

Prison Life Not For You

Well in here without a clue? Don't know what to do.

Certainly wouldn't wish it upon you.

But only me to blame, crying shame.

Can hear the rain, but wish I could smell it all the same.

In here two months at the mo', but could have a long way to go.

I'm writing because there's nothing to do, remember it could be you.

If you ever read this poem, note, letter, on the out,

Remember this ain't the way, or place to be.

They say it's easy, but it's not really, that's just what you say

To make it feel easy, 'ride it' is what we say.

Learn your's the easier way, go to school, get a job or soon just like me.

You could be under lock and key.

Drugs, stealing, any crime eventually only leads to time,

And believe me, it ain't no easy pastime. 23 hours lock up

Can you imagine, barbed wires, bars, steel doors, cold floors,

This don't make you hard at all.

Just screws you up and can make you do more.

I hope you're starting to understand the score.

'No' sometimes seems a hard word, but keep strong, it's easier than this,

Please believe me—I insist.

Crack, smack, ecstasy, cocaine, cannabis, it's all the same,

People getting rich out of misery and pain.

And even the ones who get rich and fat off our pain,

usually end up playing the jail game.

At the moment I'm 25, I hope you're younger learning from my time.

Keep the peace all the time.

The next week when I saw him again he said, 'You won't believe this, Mary, but my cellmate had a Dear John from his girlfriend last week. I talked him out of topping himself.' More mutual support.

Some time later when I saw him again he was as depressed as ever.

'My mother died last week, Mary. I just can't forgive myself, the last time she came to see me I was on at her to give up smoking. That's what killed her. But I smoke. Why couldn't I have been nicer to her? I didn't realise how ill she was. I must go to her funeral, but I couldn't bear to go in handcuffs.'

He did go, and not in handcuffs; he was given a day's parole, and returned to the prison unescorted.

This was in my early days as a QPC, before I'd started organizing silent meetings. I think Ashley would have benefited from the silence. When I first met him he was going to chapel, but after the death of his mother he stopped, 'I've lost my faith, Mary,' he said. Our silent meetings didn't require 'faith'.

Billy

I've always seen myself as a feminist, listened to, and believed women's complaints about the men in their lives. Now I was hearing the other side.

'I'm here because my wife wants me here,' said Billy, 'she told the police I'd attacked her and was hitting the children. I'd never do that, I love the children, she's the one that hits them. If they've got bruises, she puts them there. I've got a record for violence — but that's for getting into fights, always with men. I wouldn't hit a woman or a child, certainly not my own. But I get locked up awaiting trial. It's the woman they believe every time. They don't listen to the men.'

Several others agreed.

'My wife's found another man,' said Steve, 'she's got rid of me by putting me in here. I'm not even allowed to see my own children.'

The bitterness in his tone suggested this was true. Women are not blameless.

Keith

In my first few weeks in D prison I answered Keith's request to see a chaplain.

'My missus has just had a baby,' he said, and before I could congratulate him, he added, 'I want to see him.'

'I'm sure you do. Send her a VO then, why d'you need a chaplain?' I hoped he wasn't asking for baptism.

'Yes, but children can only visit parents.'

'Aren't you the parent?'

'We're not married. I need proof that I'm his dad,' he explained as if to a somewhat stupid child.

'Proof? I can't give you proof.'

'I need to be on his birth certificate. I need to sign a form.'

'Can't your girlfriend bring it in next time she comes to see you?'

'She's got to hand it in before I'm due another visit, or she'll be fined. Could you meet her somewhere outside the prison, get the form, bring it here for me to sign and take it back to her? Please.' This was the first and only time I had a request like this. I was new to the Prison Service, so I asked the newly appointed coordinating chaplain if this would be all right. He was even newer, had never worked in a prison before, we both had much to learn.

'I don't see why not,' he said.

So I met Karen in her car outside the prison, admired baby Jake, took the form to Keith's cell for him to sign, and returned it to Karen a bit later. Jake came to visit Keith regularly. For a few weeks Keith came to our meetings, but I suspect he came out of gratitude to me rather than for the silence.

Had we been discovered I could have lost my job, and probably the coordinating chaplain could have faced the sack. 'Nothing in, nothing out' is the first rule anyone working in a prison must learn. I should have learned it earlier. We must both have thought that taking the same thing in and out wouldn't count. Later it occurred to me that Karen could have forged Keith's signature, or got a friend to forge it. But I couldn't recommend forging an official document, could I?

Antony

I didn't really get to know Antony, only meeting him on a couple of occasions, and I can't now remember what took me to his cell. He was middle-aged, middle-class, a lecturer, not the sort of person you'd expect to find in a prison. His crime, which I later read about in the local paper, was growing cannabis. He only grew it for his own use, and for a friend suffering from multiple sclerosis, who found it helped the pain, and made his life bearable. However, this friend paid Antony a small sum for the drug, making Antony a 'dealer' in the eyes of the law, so he was locked-up.

What was worse than being in a cell, was knowing that when he got out he would no longer be able to grow the drug that helped his friend to live. It cost thousands of pounds to bring Antony to 'justice' and to keep him in prison. Is this really how the people of Britain want their taxes used? Why do we choose to label a drug that many find helpful in the treatment of a disease, for which there seems to be no cure, 'illegal'? How did we get into this crazy situation? More importantly how can we get back to some sanity about drugs? If drugs were decriminalised it would have a dramatic effect on the prison population: would cut re-offending at a stroke.

Jack

Jack came to prison for the first time even later in life than Antony. Jack had been a merchant seaman and plumber all his working life. In retirement, however, he found his life had lost its meaning. The only place he could find friends was the local. So he took to spending his evenings there, then also his afternoons. Soon he was drunk most evenings. On his way home he would commit various small breaches of the peace, in particular he would disturb his neighbours, by singing loudly as he opened his front door then banged it shut. They lost patience, and reported him to the police, who obtained an anti-social behaviour order (ASBO). Of course, this didn't stop his drinking or his singing. He breached the ASBO a few times before he found himself in prison.

Jack was deeply religious, and went to chapel every Sunday, as well as to our silent meetings, and to Bible study. When he was moved to C wing, with a single cell, he said, 'It's rather like the navy, Mary. I get on well with the officers, and the other prisoners. It's a tolerable life. I can cope well without alcohol in here, but what about when I get out? Where'll I spend my evenings? How can I make friends?'

He came to the silent meetings for several weeks, which he really appreciated, often speaking in the silence, usually to pray. Then he started to go to drug and alcohol meetings on a Monday afternoon.

'I'm really sorry, Mary. I miss the silence.'

'It's more important to cope with your problem with alcohol than to sit in silence,' I said.

I saw him several times after that, and he was hopeful of staying away from drink when he got out. We discussed voluntary work for the church as a way of making friends, rather than the pub, but he said he'd need CRB clearance for that. I met him a few times when he got out. On only one occasion was he drunk. I sincerely hope he managed to keep his drinking under control, or move to somewhere where the neighbours were more accepting, and I prayed that he found a way out of his loneliness. He needed a job, and although over 65 seemed to have the ability to do one, but couldn't find one; employers prefer the young. Many of those in prison mightn't be there if there were jobs to be had, to provide not just money, but comradeship, a sense of purpose and a shape to life. Once again, I wondered at the society that sent him to prison, this time for using a legal drug for support when society rejected him. So many of those in prison are there through the misuse of alcohol. Illegal drugs are less likely to lead to violence; their harm is usually only to the one taking the drug.

Daryl

Daryl was another whose problems came from alcohol. Alcoholics Anonymous came into the prison each week to help their fellow alcoholics. I heard many good reports of those who came faithfully to help other alcoholics inside. The serenity prayer was frequently quoted in our meetings and discussions:

> 'O God, grant us the serenity to accept that which cannot be changed, the courage to change that which can be changed, and the wisdom to know the one from the other, Amen.'

Daryl was full of admiration for AA.

> 'It don't matter what God it is you're praying to. It doesn't even have to be God, can be just a higher power. But you've got to accept that you can't do it on your own. That's why alcoholics keep coming to AA long after they've stopped drinking. Once an alcoholic, always an alcoholic. There's this man who comes in most weeks. He always starts, 'My name is X, and I'm an alcoholic. I last had a drink 23 years ago.'. Twenty-three years he's been coming in here to help us all that time!'

'Yes,' someone added, 'the last of AA's "Twelve Steps" is helping others.' I think this was far more widespread than just AA.

These children of God, and very many others, taught me so much over the years in B prison. There is that of God in each one, and while they may have done bad things to be sent to prison, and while there, lied to me, let me down, stole biscuits from the chapel, they were basically good people. Most had suffered as children, and at the hands of society and its punitive laws. So many kept coming back time after time, partly because, in prison, they lost so much, sometimes families, jobs, homes; they came out with a few pounds in their pockets, frequently with no one to support them. It's hardly surprising that they struggled and frequently lost. If the government really wants to reduce re-offending, it must look not only at changing offenders, but also critically at the structure of our society that leads to crime.

That I have not included any staff in this chapter is not because I don't see them as equally as children of God, but I don't have such clear memories of them. For much of the time I was often the only chaplain in the prison on Mondays, and got to meet other chaplains only at the monthly meetings. The officers and other staff are more shadowy in my memory, there in the background, often as a cause of frustration. Partly this may be because of attitudes acquired when I was a prisoner in W prison, but I think it is mainly because I saw my role as being on the side of the prisoners, there for them at a time when few others were. But officially I was there for the staff as well.

CHAPTER NINE

Lifers

'By all forgot, we rot and rot'.

Oscar Wilde, Ballad of Reading Gaol

Astonishingly some do not rot. I grew to respect those who'd survived long years in prison and yet remained human, with a sense of humour, caring for their fellows, finding a kind of freedom that makes survival possible: and enables humanity to remain intact in the face of the assault it suffers in the prison system.

B was a local prison, so we didn't have many lifers. Those who were there had mostly been recalled from D prison, and stayed for varying lengths of time.

Roger
'I didn't abscond, Mary, I just failed to return from home leave.'

'What's the difference?'

'They're very different.'

They might be different, but the result is the same: back to a closed prison, after several years in open ones.

'I wanted to see Paris. I'd never been abroad. So I went. When I got back I reported to D prison, but they sent me here.'

Why? But I asked instead, 'How did you manage to get a passport?'

'That's one of the "life skills" they taught us in D prison. When you go on home leave they give you all your property—including the passport. Seemed like a good idea to learn how to use it.'

His parole date had been approaching, when it would be decided whether he could complete his life sentence in the community rather than in prison. Roger had ruined his chance of gaining parole by that trip to Paris. Why couldn't he have waited a few months? Now it was going to be years before he would get out.

Despite having spent nearly 30 years in prison, Roger was a sensible, caring man, who seemed to me to be no threat to anyone. He'd learned to read and write in prison, gone on to get GCSEs and A-levels and was well on his way to gaining an Open University degree in social science. He came regularly to our meetings and added some depth and thoughtfulness to our discussions. I learned that D was not the first open prison he'd walked out of as his parole date came near. Then I learned that many others do something that gets them sent back to a category B prison as their parole hearing date approaches. Why? Perhaps, having spent so many years in an institution, where they didn't have to think about paying the rent, what to eat, how to spend their time, the reality of life in the world outside is terrifying. I don't believe Roger thought, 'I'd like to stay in prison. I feel safe here'. But that's what his actions seemed to be saying.

'I don't want to go to another D cat,' he said, 'they've let me down twice. I want to get my parole from here.'

I didn't like to suggest rather he'd let himself down: he wanted to believe his story. It's difficult to tell, as it changed over time; some of his stories were hard to believe. Spending so long locked up must have an effect on how one sees the truth, the difference between what is true and what one thinks is true, or would like to be true, may get confused. Prison is such an unreal way of life, reality may get lost. Roger had a vivid fantasy life; he said he'd killed his wife when he found her in bed with another man, that he'd been married twice while in prison, once to a prison nurse, once to a prison psychiatrist. These stories changed over time, once he called himself a 'double murderer'. I was sure some of his stories were fantasy. Roger's stories helped him to survive; somehow he could use fantasy as a weapon against reality. His parole hearing was held in B prison as he wanted.

He taught me about the Parole Board and its workings.

'The psychologists in D prison'll be opposing my parole, but I've got a wonderful barrister, she specialises in getting parole for long-term prisoners. She'll be able to answer psychology's case.'

Roger's partner was coming to the hearing, as was the warden of the hostel where he'd spent several home leaves and where he'd be living on release. Both would make a strong case for him to move out of prison.

I felt privileged that Roger also asked me if I'd come and speak up for him.

'I've put in a written report. I can't say more than I did in that... that you're a valuable contributor to the meetings. I can only say what I've written, and I only know you as a chaplain.'

'I'd still like your support in person.'

At first I was impressed by the Parole Board: there were three members, a judge in the chair and two lay people. The judge seemed to be fair, introducing everyone as we sat around a large oval table, making sure we could all hear. As well as Roger's barrister, his partner and the warden of the hostel, there were two psychologists from D prison, several officials from B prison, and me. The judge let Roger's barrister put her case, challenging D prison's psychologists, who didn't seem to fully understand some of the tests they'd carried out on Roger. The barrister appeared to know more about psychology than the psychologists, and was much more confident in explaining it. Then there seemed to be some confusion, the two sides seemed to be talking about something different.

'Has everyone got pages x to z in your papers?' asked the judge.

Everyone shuffled papers, eventually the barrister said, 'No.'

The hearing was adjourned while she looked at the missing pages.

'We need time to study this,' she said, 'this is important. I don't think they're using these tests right. But I need expert advice.'

She asked for the hearing to be put off to a later date. The judge agreed, although he was evidently not pleased. 'When we reconvene,' he said 'I only want one psychologist from D prison.'

I have since heard that parole hearings are frequently adjourned in this way because of sloppy paperwork, costing the public thousands. It was some time before Roger's hearing could be resumed, while the barrister studied the papers, and Roger grew more and more worried about the eventual outcome. It must have cost Roger, as well as the state, a great deal of money. He seemed to have no money problems, and had a variety of explanations for this. These included the sale of a valuable house and compensation for mistreatment in prison. Now he just wanted the hearing over

Some weeks later the Parole Board met again, but with only one woman psychologist whose evidence Roger's barrister tore apart. The tests showing that Roger was likely to be violent were unreliable for people over the age of

40. Roger was 59. The psychologist was drawing conclusions from the test results which the barrister showed couldn't be deduced from the evidence. All seemed to be going in Roger's favour, with his partner and the hostel warden saying how well he coped with life when on home leave, and promising their support when he got out. We seemed to be discussing when this would happen, not if.

However, the psychologist and one of the lay members of the Parole Board seemed far more interested in what Roger had done 30 years ago, than in the man he now was. Then the lay member started asking questions about Roger's story.

'Why did you go to Paris? You've given two conflicting stories about this: which is true?'

Roger mumbled, not making much sense.

'How did you get there? You said you went by train, but you mentioned an aeroplane, which was it?'

There was a long pause, Roger seemed flustered. 'We went by train, came back by air. I wanted to experience both,' he finally replied.

'Do you often tell lies?' asked the lay member, somewhat belligerently.

Roger was at a loss how to reply. He prevaricated. Those who knew him, were aware of his tendency to confuse fantasy and reality. But was this relevant to his threat to society? We all tell lies, particularly politicians. There are serious lies that may endanger state security, and trivial lies that make human communication run more smoothly. I felt Roger's lies, his stories, did no harm.

Then I saw that this was changing the atmosphere of the hearing. Others took up the truth telling theme, and the evidence of the psychologists seemed to be gaining ground. Here was a man who'd killed 30 years ago, and who was unreliable.

Roger was depressed by the end; his barrister was not very confident. I was allowed to take Roger to the chapel for a cup of coffee, and to eat some of the sandwiches the prison had provided for the members of the Parole Board. Despite this being far superior to his normal diet, he wasn't hungry, and was still depressed when I took him back to his cell.

Prisoners have to wait about two weeks to hear the outcome of their parole application. During this time Roger was upset and agitated, and I wasn't surprised that he felt unable to come to our meetings. Neither was I surprised that, when the Parole Board issued its report, it was recommended that he go to another open prison to prove he could be trusted. At first he said he wouldn't go, he'd rather stay in B. But eventually he agreed, and I lost touch with him. He'd promised to write to me care of the chaplaincy, and I had the governor's permission to reply, but he never wrote. One of his friends was transferred to the same prison, and he said in a letter to another friend in B that Roger was finding life hard in the new prison.

I phoned the QPC in his new prison a few times. But that prison didn't seem to welcome Quakers, and this QPC was told he could only come in if there were a Quaker prisoner. I thought Roger would be that prisoner, and the QPC would have to be admitted. But he'd never been given security clearance, and could only see Roger as a visitor. He confirmed that Roger was having problems. It seemed that he and Roger were not getting on very well, and the prison was doing nothing to make things easier.

So once again a prison relationship came to a less than satisfactory conclusion. Had it been permitted I would have made an effort to contact Roger, offered him what help I could to settle into this new prison, and eventually our relationship would have reached a natural conclusion.

Relationships made in prison are different: circumscribed, liable to come to an end without notice, at the whim of the Prison Service. Friends can be separated without warning, for any reason. It takes time to learn to negotiate these chaplaincy relationships, unique I suspect, to prison: relationships of gross inequality between one with keys, the symbol of power, and the powerless; between one held in some esteem in the community, though sometimes with some suspicion by those in power in the prison, and one rejected and derided by the community, and sometimes also by those in the prison hierarchy.

Simon

'You've been registered as of no religion, is that correct?' I asked Simon.

'It certainly isn't. I'm a Quaker.'

'So am I,' I said, interested.

'I know you are, and you have a meeting this afternoon at 2.15.'

I was slightly taken aback, he'd only been in the prison since the previous

Saturday.

'I've been recalled from D prison. Lots of my mates are here. They send us here if they think we might be going to cause a problem, or if we do.' He never told me just why he'd been sent to us.

I got to know Simon well in the time he spent with us. He was good at seeking out men who needed his support, and knowledge of prison ways. He became a faithful member of our silent meeting, frequently advising men whom he thought would benefit from it to come. The numbers at the meeting grew while Simon was with us, particularly from his wing.

I think he'd met a QPC and Quakerism in one of the many prisons he'd been in over the course of his long years in prison, as many lifers, do. At conferences of QPCs I met others who'd known him along the way. In one London prison it was Simon who'd persuaded the QPC to start a silent meeting, against his better judgement. Like me, this QPC had felt silence was not for the likes of those who filled his large category B prison. Simon proved him wrong.

'The meeting's going well. Will you thank Simon from me next time you see him' he said.

Simon was one of those who survived. For him, I hoped, becoming a Quaker helped him to remain human and caring. He became known as someone who'd help those in distress. He knew so many people in so many different prisons. He could often send a message to a man he knew in another prison, who'd be able to help another who was being sent there. It was easy to see that of God in Simon, and to watch him find it in his fellow prisoners.

Kevin

Kevin was another lifer from D prison who came to our weekly meetings. He was suffering from macular degeneration and going blind. In D prison he'd been going out each week for guide dog training, but of course that stopped as soon as he got to B prison. He was registered blind, but one of the officers questioned this, claiming he could see. He did have some remaining vision, but it was disappearing. A friend led him to collect his meals and to go to the shower, and he soon got to know his way around. B prison, like most prisons, was not designed with disabled people in mind. Kevin was soon chosen to be his wing's representative on the diversity committee. This was made up of both staff and prisoners, and dealt with complaints about racism, homophobia and other forms of discrimination, including against the disabled. Here the discrimination was in the very design of the building. Racism was something the prison fought hard against. I liked their poster picturing two brains: one large, labelled 'A Human Brain', the other small, labelled 'A Racist Brain.' However, I hoped it wasn't implying that the brains of some of those in prison are smaller than a human brain. I have seen several television programmes showing that the brain patterns of violent offenders differ from those of people with normal brains. This can be taken to imply that some people are born to be violent. I have yet to see a programme explaining that more recent research shows that abuse in childhood can change brain patterns, which can again be changed later in life.

I frequently hear people say, 'Life should mean life.' It does. Lifers in the community have many restrictions on their freedom, and can be recalled to prison for a variety of what may seem trivial reasons. Simon and Kevin, like Roger, would have to face a Parole Board before they got out. Others have told me that Parole Boards are obsessed in quite an unhealthy way with the person the man was when he committed his crime, rather than with who he has become. All lifers have to do a variety of prison courses: anger management, enhanced thinking skills, life skills and others. Why do prisons offer these courses if they don't believe people can change? All those working in the chaplaincy must believe in the possibility of transformation: it is basic to all faiths. We can submit what we see as evidence of change in a man, only to have it rejected by the risk aversion of Parole Boards.

Life sentence prisoners all have a tariff, the number of years the judge thinks they should serve before being considered for parole. All the lifers I met had served far longer than their tariff; Roger's had been 12 years, and he had been inside nearly 30. One reason for this, apart from Parole Boards' risk aversion, is that they are overwhelmed with cases needing review. This is made worse by IPP sentences: indefinite imprisonment for public protection. This sentence was brought in in 2003. Those sentenced to IPP can't be released until the Parole Board thinks they're no longer a danger to the public.

What neither the government nor the judges, with whom IPP sentences seemed popular, appeared to understand, was that the Parole Board was already overwhelmed with lifers awaiting their attention. The IPP sentence was abolished 2012, however this was not made retrospective, so that IPP prisoners awaiting release still have to wait for the Parole Board to consider their case. Prisons are still overcrowded with men whose release date has long passed, but who cannot be freed, like Eric (*Chapter 6*) who should not have died in prison at all. He'd served his two years, but the judge had made his an IPP sentence. He was dying, and obviously no threat to anyone, but he couldn't be released because the Parole Board had not seen him.

IPP sentences and life sentences that last far longer than the tariff set by the judge contribute to the overcrowding in our prisons which makes the work of helping prisoners to change so much harder. This is part of our risk averse society: nothing must pose any kind of a threat to our safety. It's better that thousands suffer injustice, costing us millions, than one person does something dreadful. We all live constantly with an infinitesimal risk of being murdered. Releasing life sentence and IPP prisoners might add marginally to that risk, and so we keep them locked-up. Can't we learn that life is a dangerous undertaking, always ending in death, and rejoice that we are alive and able to enjoy it, rather than worrying about a slight risk of a violent death that statistically will almost certainly never happen.

What is certain is that one day all of us will die, but the chance of this having anything to do with someone who once committed a crime is remote. It's far more likely to be caused by a car driver, than a released prisoner. But motoring offences seldom create the moral panics of murders or sex crimes. Newspapers encourage us to hate sex offenders, the law requires them to sign a register, parents demand to know where they live. Yet the threat of abuse to children comes, in the majority of cases, from those already known to the child: parents, step-parents, partners, carers. Fear of crime, fear of death are widespread but they can poison our lives.

As Vicky Pryce says in her book *Prisonomics* prisons cost the country millions of pounds each year. There are better ways to spend our wealth, and other ways to punish crime and reform offenders. I will look at one of these in the next chapter.

CHAPTER TEN

Restorative Justice

'Forgive us our trespasses, as we forgive those who trespass against us'.

The Lord's Prayer

I can't remember why I went to Justin's cell, perhaps to deliver a requested Bible, or some other, trivial, brief errand. I thought his name sounded familiar, and as I opened his door I remembered what I'd read about him in the local paper. I banged the bolt and went in.

'It was you who broke into my friend, the mayor's, house wasn't it?' I asked him.

'He's my friend, now.' Justin replied.

The mayor of the small town where I live had been burgled. The local paper had quoted him saying, 'I'd like to meet the person who did this to us.'

B prison was one of the first to use restorative justice (RJ). There was a graduate prison officer on the staff who'd written a dissertation on it for her degree, and was anxious to see it in use in the prison. I told her of the newspaper report, and Justin became one of her first RJ clients.

The government seems to approve of RJ: the Ministry of Justice included it in their 2013 'Victims Charter', if both parties want it. They define it thus:

'Restorative Justice is the process of bringing together those harmed by crime or conflict with those responsible for the harm, to find a positive way forward.'

I feel RJ is far more than this. It was the philosophy underlying South Africa's Truth and Reconciliation Commission. Desmond Tutu, in his book on this, *No Future Without Forgiveness*, says it's based on the African concept of *ubuntu*, which, he says, does not readily translate into English:

'It speaks of the very essence of being human...We say, "a person is a person through other people"..."I am human because I belong"...*Ubuntu* means that in a real sense even the supporters of apartheid were victims of the vicious system.'

The RJ conference which brings victims and offenders together, seeks to find out what happened, who was harmed and what can be done about it. The victim (who often feels excluded from the criminal justice system) can explain the damage done, while the offender has to take responsibility for the behaviour that caused it. Victim and offender then both discuss how to deal with the possibly disastrous aftermath, which can bring about dramatic transformation.

RJ is not the soft option it might seem to some. It asks us to take seriously the words of the Lord's Prayer to forgive and be forgiven, and understands that crime damages not just the immediate victim, but the whole of society. This is what I feel is missing from the Ministry of Justice's definition. Even the perpetrator himself or herself is harmed by the offence. RJ affirms that every individual is an essential part of the wider society, and aims, as far as is possible, to restore both victim and offender to their places in that society, and enable both to get on with their lives. Many victims find RJ helpful, in that having told the offender what their crime has meant, and hopefully heard an apology and promise of attempted restitution, they can move on, rather than remaining frozen in anger and hate. The media often seem to foster the perpetuation of this anger in high profile victims, encouraging them to see themselves as almost professional, permanent victims, encouraging them to say, 'I can never forgive this'. RJ, while acknowledging that life may never be the same for victims, nevertheless assists victims to get their lives back.

The mayor and his partner were invited into the prison to meet Justin, and were able to tell him, not only about the inconvenience of the loss of two important computers, but how the fear that someone might break into their house while they were sleeping, now kept them awake at night. The mayor's partner told how she chased Jason down the street shouting, 'All my work is on that computer, please give it back.' Justin ignored her then, dropping it as he fled. But on meeting the couple he apologised, said he was drunk, and 'out of the world' at the time. He told them that another prisoner had shown him the newspaper article, saying, 'Gosh, you stole from the mayor!' suggesting that Justin was some kind of a hero, but it affected him in quite the opposite way.

'When she came to my cell to talk about RJ, I told her I was already trying to write to the mayor,' Jason said.

'It was my partner who really got to him,' the mayor told me. 'She explained about all the months of work she'd lost on her computer.'

Jason promised to use his time in prison to get himself off drugs, and they did indeed become friends, visiting him again, giving him books, even visiting when he had been moved to another prison, some hours' drive away.

'Next time, use the front door,' they told him. Then they lost touch, but a year or two later the front doorbell rang and there was Justin, with a new wife.

'Are you working?' asked the Mayor.

'I'm her carer,' said Justin proudly, pointing to his wife, 'she's got some mental problems.'

After over an hour's talk, they parted, the mayor and his partner promising to visit Justin and his wife in their home soon.

I once borrowed a DVD on RJ and showed it to groups in the prison. Some VPs, claiming their offence didn't have victims, got angry.

'I only watched some pictures on the internet,' said Joe.

'What about the children you were watching?' I asked.

I remember the look of incomprehension on his face, 'They didn't suffer any more because I watched them.' Was he terrified of meeting the children behind those pictures?

'But the pictures wouldn't have been made if there weren't people like you wanting to watch it.'

Joe gave a shrug, suggesting total lack of empathy, an inability to understand the interrelatedness of all life, which must be the basis for successful RJ. Those who have experienced it often say that before the RJ conference they'd never considered their victims as people; meeting them, seeing them as fellow human beings can come as a shock.

Peter Woolfe in his book, *The Damage Done* says:

'I had lived my whole life cut adrift from people, living in my own little bubble, and suddenly the anger and pain of two men forced its way into me and I knew, perhaps for the very first time in my life, not only how someone else actually felt but also what that felt like for myself…I can only explain to anyone reading this, that I'd known this before, but now for the very first time in my life, I felt it. And it hurt.'

Another case of RJ originating in B prison happened shortly after I'd retired. The local Quaker meeting house was damaged in an arson attack. The arsonist, whom I never met so will call him A, was in B prison awaiting trial. The local Quakers immediately requested RJ: they needed to understand why someone had damaged their property, could they themselves have done something to make someone have a grudge against the Quakers? They knew enough about RJ to understand that it was the only way the meeting would be able to feel whole again. It was not as simple as that: initially A was pleading not guilty, so RJ wasn't possible. You can't apologise for what you didn't do. Later he changed his plea and wrote a letter of apology to the meeting, against the advice of his solicitor. I heard that A had shared a cell in B prison with someone who was attending the Quaker meetings there. Could this have had anything to do with his change of heart?

After much painstaking preparation, during which A was moved from prison to prison three times, an RJ conference took place with A, two members of the Quaker meeting, a facilitator and the local RJ coordinator. A only had his cellmate for support. In preparation for the conference the Quakers had involved the whole meeting, and took its forgiveness with them. This conference was a classic example of RJ, so much so that the local RJ coordinator wanted to video it for training purposes: it was unique in that both parties had asked for it, which is unusual, and the number of victims was unusually large. A originally agreed to this, but then said that he would like to say things he wouldn't want recorded.

At the conference, the Quakers pointed out to A that many groups who rented the meeting house had suffered while it was out of use. One of these was the local gay and lesbian community, who were worried that it might be a hate crime against them. A member of the group was one of the Quakers at the conference. A assured her he was not homophobic, in fact he's gay, on the VP wing, himself. One thing he promised to do to make amends was to write a piece about a gay man in prison for this group. The group in return offered him voluntary youth work when he got out.

The two Quakers said they would like to stay in contact with A, to find out how he was doing. He'd said his closest relationship was with his Gran.

'It'll be like having another set of Grans checking up on you,' the Quakers said. A laughed.

Oxfam lost hundreds of pounds as the weekly lunches held it the meeting house in aid of the charity had to be abandoned for several months. One member of the meeting wanted A to think of the starving children in Africa his crime had damaged. A was very contrite, and promised that when he got out he'd help at the Oxfam lunches, even if this meant wearing a pinny. He also wanted to raise money for the meeting house.

'The most important thing you can do is forgive yourself,' the Quakers told him.

This is something frequently discussed at our silent meetings, with many men saying this is the hardest part of accepting one's crime, some said they found it impossible.

'I can forgive my mum,' said Christopher (see *Chapter 8*). 'I can never forgive myself for nearly killing her.'

One of the books on the table at our meetings was *Forgiveness: Making Sense of It,* by John Phillips. A poem in that book was a favourite of Carl's who read it more than once.

Forgiveness
When the wind blows
And the sun shines
And the rainfall hits the ground;
When I breath in
And I see things
I wish I could turn it around.

I can't earn it
Don't deserve it
It won't take away the pain;
I'm not worthy
Have no power
And I wouldn't do again.

I can't ask for you to give me
The things I need to move at last
Away from all the misery and hurt
That trail forward from the past.

Whatever things need doing
I would gladly play my part,
If only you could find for me
Forgiveness in your heart.

If I could only change the world
The first thing I would do,
Is make me in a different way
So I'd never have hurt you
Forgive me.

By VH

At the end of their RJ conference both the Quakers hugged A, after asking if this would be alright, but not waiting for an answer. RJ is often seen as offering 'closure', but the Quakers said it was a beginning, rather than an end, the start of a journey, although they were not sure where this would lead. One of those involved in the conference and two other members of the area meeting were accepted to train as RJ facilitators. Problems the local meeting was suffering seemed to have been healed through working together for the RJ conference.

RJ is endorsed by the Ministry of Justice, I suspect, largely because research shows that it works. It reduces re-offending, one of the ministry's most important goals, and it is relatively cheap, particularly when compared with prison. But I worry that the ministry may be watering down the concept. RJ is at present practised mostly by those who have faith in it and understand its underlying philosophy. Now that the police, among others, are being trained in its use, and it becomes just another way of dealing with offenders, it may suffer the same fate as many innovations in education, which, when first practised, seem to have enormous benefits, for example the 'initial teaching alphabet' (through which my older daughter learned to read exceptionally quickly in the 1960s). However, when the system was rolled out as just another way of teaching reading, and the books became as dog-eared as the old ones, its advantages fell away.

Peter Woolfe describes how an RJ conference changed his life, from a career criminal to working for Restorative Solutions, touring the country with his former victim to teach about RJ. While this was a wonderful outcome for Peter, there are only so many posts for those who have been transformed to work within RJ. What RJ does is teach compassion and empathy for victims, something which those whose childhoods involved trauma and abuse may lack. Perhaps one needs more than empathy to stay away from crime. What RJ cannot do is provide work, a home, a family for offenders. To reduce re-offending we need to address the structure of society, and the inequality which breeds crime. *The Spirit Level* by Richard Wilkinson and Kate Pickett shows clearly that societies with the greatest equality consistently suffer less crime. The society damaged by the crime may itself be damaged, also in need of healing. This involves politics, which I will look at briefly it in the next chapter.

Only time will tell if RJ is able to make a real difference to the way in which we deal with criminals and their victims. It does appear to be succeeding in Northern Ireland where it is a standard part of their youth justice system. Here it is gaining acceptance for less serious crimes, although research has shown it to be as effective with crimes of violence.

Amid financial cutbacks, prison chaplaincies, with their own resources increasingly limited, continue to try to 'celebrate the goodness of life.' RJ is an essential part of this. The Quakers' experience with A shows, once again, that good can come out of evil.

CHAPTER ELEVEN

Positive Justice

'If only there were evil people somewhere insidiously committing evil deeds, and it were necessary only to separate them from the rest of us and destroy them. But the line dividing good and evil runs through the heart of every human being and who is willing to destroy a piece of his own heart?'

Alexander Solzhenitsyn, *The Gulag Archipelago 1918–1956* (1973)

As I got to know more and more children of God in B prison, I realised increasingly that there is good and evil in all of us, however much the popular press insist that certain people are 'evil' and need to be incarcerated. I first heard these words of Solzhenitsyn in February 2008 at a conference of Quakers in Criminal Justice entitled 'From Faith to Action'. They were quoted by Marina Cantacuzino of the Forgiveness Project; this explores concepts of forgiveness, and encourages people to consider alternatives to resentment, retaliation and revenge. Another speaker at the conference was Juliet Lyon of the Prison Reform Trust, who reported a meeting with Jack Straw, then justice secretary. He'd said to her that week when she made some suggestion, 'That would be an excellent idea, Juliet, but how would it run in the *Daily Mail?*'

I think all of us at that conference were incensed to think that the government believes the views of the *Daily Mail* are public opinion. Juliet Lyon reported that surveys carried out by the Prison Reform Trust show that people are far less vindictive than that paper. Perhaps our views of human beings are more in line with Solzhenitsyn's. The conference ended with a challenge to put the ideas of the speakers into action. Working in B prison I had been wondering increasingly if it was enough to try to help those damaged by our society. We need also to work for change in the system to ensure this damage doesn't occur, and to oppose views like those of the *Daily Mail*.

The purposes of the modern penal system are generally supposed to include: retribution, showing society's rejection and abhorrence of the crime, deterring others from committing crime and the reform of the wrongdoer, so that they don't offend in the future. These frequently conflict: deterrent or retributive sentences can make reform harder. The emphasis on the reform of the criminal seemed to be most important in dealing with crime in the post-war period. With the death penalty abolished, in the face of public support for it, and beating of prisoners ended, new and more humane ways of dealing with offenders were being tried. There has been a change back to retribution and deterrence since around the end of the 20th-century in the minds of legislators and the media alike. A culture of vengeance seems to pervade our society, as sentences inexorably grow longer. This is supposed to reflect public demand for 'tougher sentences', yet as the Prison Reform Trust's research suggests, the public, if asked, would often suggest shorter sentences than those imposed by the courts. Yet we continue to send people to prison for ever longer, with prisons increasingly overcrowded making reform or rehabilitation increasingly problematic, and we seem satisfied to lock-up more offenders per head of population than any other European country. Our media call for longer and longer sentences for those we choose to label 'criminal', and justice secretaries of all parties comply.

Prisons exist because our democratic society wants them: it's important that we know just what goes on in them, and why, and the fact that in many cases prison does not work. Louis Blom-Cooper demonstrates in *The Penalty of Imprisonment: Why Sixty Per Cent of the Prison Population Should Not Be There,* that prisons are, in most cases, '... at best ineffective and at worst counterproductive ... it is hard to find informed observers of criminal justice who believe that this level of imprisonment is either necessary or desirable.'

The Prison Reform Trust's Bromley Briefing for 2013 says, 'The trend in average sentence lengths has been increasing, they are now 2.7 months longer than in 2002'. Financial stringency means that many courses, classes and innovations found to be reducing re-offending have ended; retribution or revenge as the motive for imprisonment seems now to reign supreme. Amid all this, prison chaplaincies continue to try to 'contribute to the care of prisoners to enable them to lead law-abiding and useful lives in custody and after release.'

From time to time much of our popular press take the chance to scream about 'evil' individuals, often the parents of a child or baby horribly hurt or killed by the wickedness of parents. The innocence and helplessness of the child is contrasted with the horror that is the parents. Yet if these children survive, they may grow up to become such monsters themselves, may join the one in three of the over 80,000 people now in prison who were in care as children. I met many men whose childhoods were a catalogue of neglect and abuse (see *Chapter 8*, Sean and Jason). At what age does society's vociferous concern for the welfare of the innocent child turn to fear and loathing when that child grows up to be a 'hoody', a thug, a drug-dealer? The very same papers that denounced those who failed to care for the innocent baby, are soon demanding incarceration of the teenager or adult that baby has become.

It's easy to see that of God in a small baby, even for those who, unlike myself, believe in original sin. When does this vanish? Why can't we see it in those whose childhoods were rejection and abuse by parents who, in all probability, had known nothing different when they themselves were young?

One of the Quakers who came to the prison meetings had at one time run a restaurant. He said he tried to employ ex-offenders. In fact Spenser recognised him, 'My sister used to work for you,' he said.

The Friend remembered her. He told the meeting that his employees frequently abused his trust, and he would find them stealing from his kitchen.

'For many it was hard to give up old ways,' he said, 'but I always said to them, "I'm disappointed in you, but I want to give you a second chance". They always took that chance, and never stole again.'

We are an unforgiving society and offer few second chances. Couldn't we be more understanding of the environment so many in prison come from, and make allowances, offering treatment rather than punishment? Young people make up a disproportionate number of those in custody; often inappropriate use of drugs or alcohol is to blame. When students at Oxford University get drunk, and perhaps smash up a restaurant, they can go on to become prime minister. Such behaviour in the less privileged can lead to a life of crime, much of it spent in prison.

Perhaps we need to legislate against another form of discrimination. We have laws against discrimination on the ground of sex, race, sexuality, disability. Could we extended this to criminal records? The fact that someone coming out of prison has to disclose their record makes it extremely hard to find a job, somewhere to live, or insurance on their house or car. It's hardly surprising that so many return to prison. If they lie to get a job, as Carl did in *Chapter 8*, they are immediately dismissed when this is discovered. If they could be allowed a fresh start, a second chance, there might be fewer people behind bars.

RJ discussed in the previous chapter may lack the appeal of revenge. I suspect one needs to experience it to understand just how hard it can be, yet RJ, as its title implies, involves an attempt to restore the situation, in so far as this is possible, to what it was before the offence. Surely this is more important than simply showing society's abhorrence of the crime. Retribution, in the public eye, seems largely to be seen in terms of vengeance, 'an eye for an eye,' which, as Gandhi said, 'leaves the whole world blind.'

The challenge of that conference in 2008 decided for me that we need local groups to oppose and question the views of the *Daily Mail*, and other media; to put across positive ideas of human beings, and support and report what positive work can be and is being done in the penal system, so that the good within individuals may be helped to flourish. Working initially with local Quakers, then with others of any faith and none I helped to establish a Positive Justice (PJ) group in my own county. Its aims, agreed after long discussions with the committee, were to:

- Encourage the use of restorative and therapeutic practices within the criminal justice system, in order to reduce crime and its impact on victims.

- Act as a pressure group: balancing negative representations in the popular press, and raising public awareness of, and support for, positive initiatives within the criminal justice system, particularly alternatives to imprisonment where appropriate.

To try to achieve these we agreed to:

- Organize regular public meetings, and informal discussion forums;

- Disseminate accurate and up to date information regarding crime and the community;

- Cooperate with other community/voluntary groups;

- Act as an information point for those who wish to get involved with the voluntary sector;

- Act as an information point for those who wish to get involved with the voluntary sector;

- Promote positive policies to the media and to policymakers by writing letters, putting out press releases and through our website.

Our first public meeting was held during Prisons Week in November 2008 with Erwin James, *Guardian* columnist, author of *A Life Inside* and a life sentence prisoner now on life licence, as the main speaker. The title was 'Crime and Punishment—Where's the Justice?' This was followed by a panel discussion. We used the media to advertise this meeting; an interview with Erwin and the 'Ealing Vicarage rape victim', who was one of the panel, was broadcast on local radio. I'm sure this helped to swell our audience for the meeting, which was held in a hall of the local university, and attracted about 140, largely students. We were delighted that many of these students seemed to echo the views of the *Daily Mail*, asking questions such as, 'Why should they have a pool table in the prison?' and 'Why do prisoners get their education free when we have to pay.' I hope Erwin's answers and those of the panel made them at least think about the subject.

PJ try to hold a public meeting each year in Prisons Week, and with one exception, where we unfortunately clashed with Children in Need, these have been well attended. In 2010 we invited Baroness Corston to speak on 'Women in Prison'; she had recently published an influential report on the subject. This meeting attracted an audience of around 80. That year we also cooperated with another local group to ask Professor David Nutt to speak on 'War on Drugs—Time for Peace?'. He'd lost his job as the government's adviser on drugs, for questioning the harm done by illegal substances, and claiming that alcohol is the most dangerous drug. In 2011 we hired the Forgiveness Project exhibition for a week and staged it in the local cathedral. We also held a meeting with Tim Newell of 'Escaping Victimhood', which provides supportive residential workshops for people whose lives have been disrupted by serious crime, especially murder and manslaughter.

In 2012 we ran a debate on the motion, 'This house believes that prison works.' A prison governor and an ex-prisoner proposed this; it was opposed by Juliet Lyon, of the Prison Reform Trust and a local MP. This attracted well over 100 people in a local comprehensive school, with several school students in the audience. One of these said, 'Before this evening my views on crime were fairly standard, I didn't like criminals, and wanted them locked-up. But having heard the speakers I'm thinking again.' This is exactly what we wanted the debate to achieve. The motion was heavily defeated, but the chair allowed a second vote on 'This house believes that prison could work,' which was overwhelmingly carried.

Our 2013 meeting was again held in the university, with Ben Gunn as speaker. Ben spent 32 years in prison for killing a school friend. He rang the police as soon as he realised what he'd done, and one might have thought he would be found guilty only of manslaughter. But he was sentenced to life for murder, with a tariff of ten years. He told us that it was his rebellion that kept him in so long, and kept his sanity; he refused to cooperate with the prison system. The Parole Board, yet again, chose not to look at the person he had become. He had gained a masters degree and was two years into a PhD when released.

As well as public meetings, PJ holds twice yearly lunchtime forums, where people are invited to bring food to share, and discuss a variety of criminal justice-related topics. The first of these was on restorative justice, and I like to think the letters we were urged to write helped in the campaign to get this into B prison. The prison officer working there, who wanted RJ in the prison (see previous chapter) spoke, with Nigel Whiskin of Restorative Solutions. One of our forums was a picnic on a wonderful sunny Saturday in July 2013, when several ex-prisoners shared their experiences of coming out of prison, and the problems they faced. All agreed it was hard to know where to go for help to find answers to simple questions such as, 'How do you get on a doctor's list?' One, a lifer still in D prison, on his day out, said he didn't even know the questions to ask. At another such meeting Kate Cairns, of Kate Cairns Associates, spoke on 'Beyond Reason—Addressing the Roots of Criminal Behaviour'. Here we learned not only how important trauma and abuse can be in setting a child, particularly a vulnerable child, out on a life of crime and violence, but also how it's possible to change the life of that child through the developing their resilience. Other meetings included: the arts in prison, children in custody, the Alternatives to Violence Project, victims of crime, growing old in prison.

We enjoyed music and talk from 'Changing Tunes' a group, that encourages the latent talent of prisoners in making music. We held a discussion on the government green paper 'Breaking the Cycle—Effective Punishment, Rehabilitation and Sentencing of Offenders,' and drafted a PJ response.

Hopefully we are helping local people to become more informed and thoughtful about crime and punishment. We try, as our title suggests, to give support to positive initiatives, including RJ, a topic to which we are returning, with a forum where the Quakers already mentioned and an ex-offender, now a restorative justice facilitator, will speak. Over just a few years RJ is rapidly gaining acceptance, rather than being something no one has heard of. So many of the children of God I met in B prison had been damaged by society and so little seems currently to be being done to heal them. We must change society's attitudes.

CHAPTER TWELVE

Conclusion: Children of God

'We are all meant to shine as children do. It's not just in some of us; it is in everyone. And as we let our own lights shine, we unconsciously give other people permission to do the same. As we are liberated from our own fear, our presence automatically liberates others'.

Nelson Mandela, quoting Marianne Williamson's *A Return to Love*

In my ten years in B prison I didn't meet a single person who wasn't 'meant to shine'. What else did I learn there? It would be easy to say I learned 'There but for the grace of God go I.' But I never think of God as a being who could distribute grace so arbitrarily. I was lucky to have been born into a loving middle-class family, so that the rebellion of my school days didn't get labelled 'juvenile delinquency', and didn't lead me into the criminal justice system.

The children of God in B prison, whatever their faults, often seemed so caring. I witnessed empathy in so many post-silence discussions. I think they had *ubuntu* (see *Chapter 10*), the ability to see what it means to be human. This basic unity of all life became more and more real to me. My faith in the Inner Light was immensely strengthened by meeting these men, but I also came to see that the unity of all life involves sharing one another's evil as well as good.

'Yield yourself and all your outward concerns to God's guidance so that you may find "the evil weakening in you and the good raised up"', says *Quaker Advice* No. 9, quoting George Fox. We must lead our lives in, and base our relationships on, the Inner Light, on that of God in everyone we meet. Again quoting George Fox we must 'answer that of God' in them. But the darkness also is real, and can be seen in damaged lives. Christopher (see *Chapter 8*) needed to believe in his demons, who tormented him in the silence. I came to realise not just that he needed them to survive, but that we all have our shared demons. There is inner darkness as well as inner light.

Shortly after retiring from B prison, I went on holiday to Poland and visited Auschwitz. Here I saw the grim reality of evil. After 70 years it was palpable in those prison blocks with their piles of artificial limbs, children's toys and fabric woven from human hair.

'What does it do to you,' I asked our young guide, 'showing visitors this horror day after day?'

'It is hard, but it is necessary,' she replied.

It is necessary, if we are all truly to be part of mankind, to acknowledge that being human includes the depths to which we can sink, as well as the heights to which we can rise; our sordid failings, as well as our infinite possibilities and the eternal promise that what might be could be. Perhaps my understanding of what it is to be human is now more realistic, less sentimentally idealistic. I am not comparing the men in B prison with gas chamber operatives, but I think I see, now, how such evil, if nourished, could flourish. At the same time I saw that however low they may have fallen, no one is outside the web of life, beyond redemption. This must be the most important message I learned, the message of Quakerism, of all Christianity, and of other faiths. William Noblett, in his book *Prayers for People in Prison* writes, 'At the heart of each person who ministers in a prison, there is a faith rooted in the reality and purpose of God, in whom all things are possible.'

My belief in the truth of all faiths, was deepened by working with chaplains with other beliefs, and their followers. I hope I became more tolerant of those I disagreed with quite profoundly. Karen Armstrong in her book, *The Battle for God,* writes that Buddhists, Taoists, Hindus and monotheists agree that the sacred reality is not simply transcendent 'out there', but is 'enshrined in every single human being who must therefore be treated with absolute honour and respect.' Christians believe that all are created in the image of God, Quakers go further, we testify to that of God in all: God within, not an image. An image can be destroyed, that of God cannot.

Increasingly I found I could accept the reality of a God beyond the God in each individual: more than the sum of all the individual inner lights. Scientists tell us we are all made up of more than 90 per cent water, with some essential chemicals: the rest is 'star stuff', and comes from the Big Bang. Through this we are 'meant to shine'.

I could see this shining potential also in those whom even prisoners revile, and recognised just how much we all share with them. All are part of the great web of life. As John Donne said, 'Any man's death diminishes me, because I am involved in mankind.' So equally, everyone's life impacts on me. We all share the common good and the common evil; the darkness and the light; the life and the death.

The prison chaplain walks a tightrope, working for prison staff and prison inmates. I know I largely failed in relationships with staff, partly perhaps because I felt myself too much in sympathy with prisoners, I possibly felt some identification with, the children of God without the keys. Perhaps the memory of having once, however briefly, been one of them (*Chapter 4*) still runs deep in my psyche. I should have made a greater effort to answer that of God in the staff. Where I had differences of opinion with them, it was usually because they had a job to do, rules to follow and perhaps a different agenda in coping with the people we demand be locked-up, and locked-up securely, sometimes for life.

I was appointed QPC by my area meeting, and was in B prison as their representative, so I tried to involve that meeting in the work of the prison. Friends from the area meeting came to the prison meeting. I gave reports of my work to area meetings, seeing the work in B prison as part of the work of the meeting. I don't think I was very successful in this. Several Friends said they found my reports interesting, but on one occasion the clerk asked me to limit myself to five minutes, as there was a great deal of important business to get through. Some in the meeting didn't share my view that the work in the prison was one of the more important pieces of business we had.

I hope I now see more clearly the Inner Light in all those I meet; acknowledging the darkness doesn't make this harder. As George Fox wrote, 'I saw also that there was an ocean of darkness and death, but an infinite ocean of light and love which flowed over the ocean of darkness.' Or, as St. John's Gospel puts it, 'The light shines ... and the darkness has never been able to put it out.' This is perhaps my most profound lesson, and, again in the words of George Fox, I learned it 'experimentally', meaning through experience. This is a truth I shall try and live the rest of my life by.

I continue to hold more strongly my belief in the ability of individuals to change; but if we are to reduce re-offending society needs to change, as well as individuals. I shall for ever be grateful to my area meeting for giving me the privilege of working in B prison, and to the children of God I met there.

Bibliography

Aitken, Jonathan (2000) *Pride and Perjury*, London: Harper Collins

Armstrong, Karen (2000) *The Battle for God, Fundamentalism in Judaism, Christianity and Islam*, London: Harper Collins

Beckford, James A, and Gilliat, Sophie (1998) *Religion in Prison—Equal Rites in a Multi-faith Society*, Oxford: Blackwell

Bidder, Jane (2010) *The Book of Uncommon Prayer*, Warrington: Bar None books

Blom-Cooper, Louis (2008) *The Penalty of Imprisonment—Why Sixty Percent of the Prison Population Shouldn't Be There*, London: Continuum

Brown, Mary (2002) *Inside Art*, Sherfield on Loddon: Waterside Press

Cairns, Kate (2006) *Attachment, Trauma and Resilience*, London: BAAF

Cairns, Kate, *Circles of Harm: Surviving Paedophilia and Network Abuse*, London: BAAF

Faivre, Daniel, and McCaffry, Tony (eds.) *Transcendence—Prayer of People of Faith*, Hounslow: Brother Daniel Favre, S.G.

Gillman, Harvey (1997) *A Light That is Shining—An Introduction to the Quakers*, London: Quaker Books

James, Erwin (2003) *A Life Inside*, London: Atlantic Books

Lacout, Pierre (1985) *God is Silence*, London: Quaker books

Miller, Maureen, (2009) *A Heart to Help—An Introduction to the Work of Quaker Prison Chaplains*, Hardshaw and Mann Area Meeting

Newell, Tim and Edgar, Kimmett (2006) *Restorative Justice in Prisons*, Sherfield on Loddon: Waterside Press

Noblett, William (1998) *Prayers for People in Prison*, Oxford: Oxford University Press

Nutt, David (2012) *Drugs Without the Hot Air: Minimising the Harms of Legal and Illegal Drugs*, Cambridge Uit Cambridge Limited (from the we)

Phillips, John (2010) *Forgiveness: Making Sense of It*, Banstead: Beacon Light

Prison Reform Trust (2013) *Bromley Briefings Prison Factfile*

Pringle, Peter (2012) *About Time: Surviving Ireland's Death Row*, Dublin: The History Press

Pryce, Vicky (2013) *Prisonomics: Behind Bars in Britain's Failing Prisons,* London: Biteback Publishing

Rose, June (1980) *Elizabeth Fry,* London: Macmillan

Tutu, Desmond (1999) *No Future Without Forgiveness,* London: Rider

Wilkinson, Richard and Pickett, Kate (2009) *The Spirit Level,* London: Penguin

Woolf, Peter (2008) *The Damage Done,* London: Bantam Press

Yearly Meeting of the Religious Society of Friends (1995) *Quaker Faith and Practice,* London, Yearly Meeting of the Religious Society of Friends

Yearly Meeting of the Religious Society of Friends (2008) *Advices and Queries,* London, Yearly Meeting of the Religious Society of Friends (Quakers) in Britain

Organizations referred to in *Confessions of a Prison Chaplain*

Alternatives to Violence Project: www.avpbritain.org.uk

Changing Tunes: www.changingtunes.org.uk

Circles of Support and Accountability: www.circles-uk.org.uk

Escaping Victimhood: www.escapingvictimhood.com

Jews in Prison: www.jewsinprison.org/story

Kate Cairns Associates: www.katecairns.com

Koestler Trust: www.koestlertrust.org.uk

Phoenix Prison Project: www.theppt.org.uk

Prison Reform Trust: www.prisonreformtrust.org.uk

Quakers in Criminal Justice: www.qicj.org

Restorative Solutions: www.restorativesolutions.org.uk

Index

Inside Art: Crime, Punishment and Creative Energies
by Mary Brown

This stimulating work is based on conversations with artists—including people in prison or who were once imprisoned. It charts the importance of creative activity as an instrument of personal change.

Paperback | ISBN 978-1-872870-89-2

2001 | 144 pages